The dyaloge called Funus

&

The Epicure

VOLUME III OF THE PUBLICATIONS

OF THE RENAISSANCE ENGLISH TEXT SOCIETY

The dyaloge called Funus

A Translation of Erasmus's Colloquy

(1534)

&

A very pleasaunt
& fruitful Diologe called
The Epicure

Gerrard's Translation of Erasmus's Colloquy

(1545)

EDITED BY ROBERT R. ALLEN

Published for

The Newberry Library

by

The University of Chicago Press

Standard Book Number: 226-21483-4

Library of Congress Catalog Card Number 79-92771

THE UNIVERSITY OF CHICAGO PRESS, CHICAGO 60637
The University of Chicago Press, Ltd., London

Contents

The dyaloge called Funus

Facsimile of block on title page of the Low German translation of *Funus*
(Magdeburg, 1531). Original, 64 × 70 mm. Courtesy of the Herzog August
Bibliothek, Wolfenbüttel.

Introduction

The earliest known English translation of a colloquy by
Erasmus survives in a single copy, wanting its first leaf. In
the absence of a title page, the piece takes the title from the
explicit that follows the text of the colloquy: *ẙ dyaloge called
Funus.*[1] Apparently the piece was not recorded at the time
Henry de Vocht edited reprints of five other Erasmian colloquies in 1928.[2] In 1960 it emerged from a private collection
and was purchased by the British Museum. Through their
article, "Three Sixteenth-Century English Translations of
Erasmus in a Contemporary Binding," which described *The
dyaloge called Funus* and its two companion-pieces, A. F.
Allison and H. M. Nixon heightened the attention that came
to the acquisition.[3] One purpose of the present reprint, then,
is to advance the general project begun by De Vocht: to
make the known sixteenth-century translations of the colloquies of Erasmus available to present-day readers. A second
and related purpose in setting forth this edition is to express
my appreciation of qualities belonging to the dialogue itself.
I subscribe to Craig R. Thompson's estimate of its literary
merits—that *Funus* is among the best of the colloquies.[4]

1. Sig. D2. Except in transcription of the colophon (below, p. 11), the
abbreviation 'ẙ' is hereafter expanded and printed 'the' or 'The'.

2. In *The Earliest English Translations of Erasmus' Colloquia*, Humanis-
tica Lovaniensia, no. 2 (Louvain, 1928), De Vocht published five colloquies
under their four sixteenth-century titles.

3. *British Museum Quarterly*, XXIII (1960–61), 59–63. Besides ac-
knowledging my debt to the authors for these guiding observations, I add
my thanks to Mr. Nixon for his answers to particular questions about the
book.

4. I am grateful to Professor Thompson for permission to record a spoken remark that he made to this effect. Also, see the headnote in his translation, *The Colloquies of Erasmus* (Chicago and London, 1965), p. 358.

THE LATIN COLLOQUY AND THE ENGLISH TRANSLATION

Funus was one of four new dialogues in the edition of the *Colloquia Familiaria* printed at Basel by Johannes Froben in February 1526.[5] Eight years later, less a month, Robert Copland printed the English translation. For the interval there is record of twenty-eight other Latin editions of collected *Colloquia* containing *Funus;* three of these are not cited in *Bibliotheca Belgica.*[6] For the same span of years, six editions of selected *Colloquia* are recorded; only one of them contains *Funus.*[7] I have compared twenty-seven of these thirty known texts of *Funus.*[8]

New substantive Latin readings enter the stream of texts in the edition printed at Basel by Jerome Froben and Nicho-

---

5. For a description of this edition, see *Bibliotheca Belgica,* ed. F. van der Haeghen, 2d ser., VIII–XI (Ghent, 1891–1923)—hereafter cited as *BB* —no. E460. See also Preserved Smith, *A Key to the Colloquies of Erasmus,* Harvard Theological Studies, XIII (Cambridge, Mass., 1927), pp. 39–43.

6. In *BB,* see E460–E464, E466–E473, E475, E477–E480, E482–E483, E485–E490. *Bibliographie Lyonnaise,* ed. H. L. Baudrier, 12th ser. (Paris, 1895–1921), XII, 306, lists an edition printed at Lyon by Johann Klein in 1530. (I cite it hereafter with reference to *BB* as [E476ᵇⁱˢ].) The edition printed at Lyon by Sebastian Greyeff (Gryphius) in 1533 (copies in Bibliothèque Nationale and University of Chicago Library) may be designated *BB* [E487ᵇⁱˢ]. An edition printed at Lyon by Johann Klein (a copy at University of Illinois Library) appears to bear the date 1534 printed in the title page and the colophon. Both dates appear to be altered by hand in ink to 1544. Because of these features, and because the contents are complete only with respect to the colloquies added in the edition of September 1529, the earlier date for the printing may be the actual one. The copy may be a piece of old stock unloaded at the later date. I cite the edition tentatively, therefore, as *BB* [E490ᵇⁱˢ].

7. It is the *Varia Colloquia,* printed at Paris by Robert Estienne in 1529 (copies in the Vatican Library and University of Illinois Library). (In keeping with *BB,* the edition takes the number [E645ᵇⁱˢ].) Selections of *Colloquia* not containing *Funus* are *BB,* E465, E474, E476, E481, and E484.

8. I have not succeeded in viewing a copy of three editions: in *BB,* E470 —copy cited in Bibliothèque de l'Université, Louvain, and reported lost; [E476ᵇⁱˢ]—copy cited in Baudrier collection, not located; E488—one copy cited in Biblioteca Nacional, Madrid, reported lost, and another copy, in Bibliothèque de Tournai, destroyed.

las Episcopius in September 1531. Six other texts carry them. Because the translator renders them into English, the readings isolate a group of seven texts as possible editions from which he worked.[9] The English translations of these Latin readings are[10]—

1. neyther here was ony other thynge *for* nec hic alia res erat *seven texts instead of* nec ∧ alia res erat *twenty other texts*
2. the moost inferyour place, that was to go the formest *for* locum . . . infimum, hoc est primum *instead of* locum . . . infimum ∧
3. to be of a quyet mynde *for* quieto esse animo *instead of* forti esse animo
4. eyther to bereue ony man his merytes *for* uel meritis quenquam suis spoliare *instead of* uel meritis ∧ suis spoliare

Directional evidence, albeit slender, suggests that *BB*, E479 was the edition the translator used. Four readings—two involving prefixes and two with dropped words—weaken the candidacy of the six other editions in the group of seven.

9. The seven texts (place of printing, printer, date, and copies seen) are *BB*, E479 (Basel: Jerome Froben and Nicholas Episcopius, September 1531; Bibliothèque Nationale; Bibliotheek van de Rijksuniversiteit, Ghent; and Bayerische Staatsbibliothek, Munich [a copy cited by *BB* at Reims is reported as not found; Dessau copy destroyed]); E482 (Cologne: Johannes Gymnicus, 1532; Folger Library); E483 (Basel: Jerome Froben and Nicholas Episcopius, March 1533; Bodleian Library); E485 (Lyon: Melchior and Gaspar Trechsel, 1533; Bibliothèque Municipale, Orléans; and University of Illinois Library); E486 (Cologne: Johannes Gymnicus, 1533; Universitäts- u. Stadtbibliothek, Cologne; and Koniklijke Bibliotheek, The Hague); E487 ([Paris: François?] Gryphius, 1533; Bibliotheek van de Rijksuniversiteit, Ghent); and E489 (Cologne: Johannes Gymnicus, 1534; Sächsische Landesbibliothek, Dresden). Because *BB* describes E488 as "exemplaire de l'édition" E487, what is said below of readings in E487 must be supposed of E488.

10. All passages from *Funus* in this introduction are quoted from *BB*, E479. For convenience of reference, the locations of corresponding passages in *Des. Erasmi Opera omnia*, ed. J. Clericus (Leiden, 1703–6; reprinted, Hildesheim, 1961–62)—hereafter cited as Leiden edition—are also given. (Leiden edition has differences of spelling, punctuation, capitalization, and abbreviation.) Compare *The dyaloge called Funus*, pp. 36 and 42, with E479, sigs. Y2, Y2ᵛ, and Y6; Leiden edition, I, 814A, 814C, and 816B. I use inferior carets to show the point at which Latin passages differ.

First, although the casual use of the prefixes *per* and *pro* in other writings of the period dictates against making distinctions based upon them, the English phrase "in the whiche was graunted" seems more properly a translation of the reading *in quo permittebatur* (found in E479, E482, E486, E487, and twenty other texts) as opposed to *in quo promittebatur* (E483, E485, and E489).[11] Second, the phrase "wherin was promysed to George" appears to translate *quibus Georgio promittebatur* (E479, E483, E485, E487, E489, and twenty other texts), not *quibus Georgio permittebatur* (E482 and E486).[12] Third, the phrase "onely thretnyng them very cruelly" is a translation of *dira tantum minitantes* (E479, E483, E487, and E489), not ∧ *tantum minitantes* (E482 and E486), and not *dira* ∧ *minitantes* (twenty other texts).[13] Fourth, the phrase "in all his lyfe tyme" corresponds with *in omni uita* (E479 and twenty-five other texts), not *in* ∧ *vita* (E487 only).[14] That is, in each of the six other editions in the group there is at least one accidental reading that makes it less likely than E479 to have been the source for the translation.

Five translations of *Funus*—in a total of eight recorded editions—appeared in languages other than English before 1534. There were two translations in Spanish, one in Low German, and two in High German.[15] Three interesting similarities exist between *The dyaloge called Funus* and certain of these editions. First, the Low German and the later High German translation incorporate a passage from *De utilitate*

11. *The dyaloge called Funus*, p. 36; E479, sig. Y2; E483, sig. M2; Leiden edition, I, 814B, reads *in quo promittebatur*.

12. *The dyaloge called Funus*, p. 37; E479, sig. Y2ᵛ; E482, sig. 2H2; Leiden edition, I, 814C–D.

13. *The dyaloge called Funus*, p. 31; E479, sigs. X6–6ᵛ; E482, sig. 2G7; Leiden edition, I, 812B.

14. *The dyaloge called Funus*, p. 45; E479, sig. Y8ᵛ; E487, sig. N8; Leiden edition, I, 817B.

15. For descriptions see *BB*, E750, E751–E752 (new editions of the translation printed in E750), E753, E777, E778 (a revised edition of E777), E789, and E795. I have examined the text of a copy of each of these editions except E750 and E751. The woodcut from the title page of E795 is reproduced in this edition, p. 2.

Colloquiorum as their "Argument."[16] Second, two editions of the earlier High German text gloss the name "Phaedrus" as "pulcher."[17] Third, the translation of the phrase *Militibus Germaniae* in the Low German and three editions of the two High German versions gives variant spellings of a word cognate with the English reading, "To the landeskneyghtes of Germany."[18] These common features, however, seem as likely to be the result of chance as of influence. That is, they do not afford the conclusion that the English translator consulted any one of the texts in a vernacular language.

With respect to its Latin model, the English translation of 1534 is complete, sequential, and literal. In a few places, however, the translation offers no English equivalent for a word or short expression in the Latin text. These omissions are probably accidental. Their effect is slight. For example, the exclamation *Phy* and the adverbial phrase *ut fit* receive no counterparts.[19] The phrase *ad flumen* does not find its way into the English list of places where despairing men are said to end their lives.[20] The translation adheres to the order of the Latin

16. Compare *BB*, E795, sigs. A2–A2ᵛ, and E789, sig. A1ᵛ, with E479, sigs. 2S2–2S2ᵛ, Leiden edition, I, 906B–C, and *The dyaloge called Funus*, p. 21.

17. Compare *BB*, E777, sig. A2ᵛ, and E778, sig. A3, with *The dyaloge called Funus*, p. 23.

18. Compare E479, sig. Y3; Leiden edition, I, 814D; E795, sig. B8, "Den landes knechten"; E778, sig. B4ᵛ, "den landtssknechten"; E789, sig. B8ᵛ, "Den Landtsknechten"; *The dyaloge called Funus*, p. 37. "Lansknyght" (1530) and "Launcekneyghtes" (1550), the two contemporary forms that the *Oxford English Dictionary* records, are further from the German readings.

19. For both see E479, sig. X7; Leiden edition, I, 812D. Compare *The dyaloge called Funus*, p. 31, where, if translated, they would occur.

20. E479, sig. X2ᵛ; Leiden edition, I, 810D. Compare *The dyaloge called Funus*, p. 25. For other places at which the Latin and English are not point-for-point, compare *et quintum Cartusiensium* (E479, sig. Y2ᵛ; Leiden edition, I, 814D) with "and ∧ of the Charter monkes" (*The dyaloge called Funus*, p. 37). Compare *Caetera Marcolphe non audeo referre* (E479, sigs. X5–5ᵛ; Leiden edition, I, 811E) with "To tell the what was more spoken I dare not" (*The dyaloge called Funus*, p. 29), where the nominative of address is omitted. Compare, also, *Catarinae Senensi* (E479, sig. X8; Leiden edition, I, 813A) with "to saynt Katheryn" (*The dyaloge called Funus*, p. 33), where the name of the place associated with the saint is dropped. Compare

speeches and to the order of clauses within them. It pursues the syntax of Erasmus—sometimes to the point of awkwardness. For example, the passage "This request hardly, but at the length with intreatynge of the wyfe and certayn of his kynsmen was opteyned" serially reproduces *Id aegre quidem, sed tandem blanditiis uxoris ac propinquorum impetratum est.*[21] With equal faithfulness, "And afterwarde other sholde doo soo lykewyse, lest ony rumour or besynesse sholde be for the same" follows *post hoc caeteri quoque fortirentur, ne quid hinc oriretur tumultus.*[22] At the remove of four centuries, the literal readings that characterize the translation sound rugged, but right. Typical of many homely passages, "All these maters fynysshed, the wyfe and the chyldren gaue theyr ryght handes to the seke man. sweryng that they shold obserue that thyng whiche they had receyued" is the plain-faced equivalent of its Latin: *His peractis, uxor et liberi datis dextris aegroto, iurant se seruaturos quod recepissent.*[23] The frequency with which English words are borrowed from Latin ones heightens our sense of this literal quality. For example, just as "transfigured and afflate with a new spirite" reflects *transfigurari afflarique nouo spiritu,* so "I sayd Vincentius, am a bacheler of dyuynyte formate / and shortly shall be lycentyate" mirrors *Ego, inquit Vincentius, sum sacrae theologiae baccalaureus formatus, mox licentiandus.*[24]

When the translation departs from the Latin text, it is usually in order to be more explicit. At their least venturesome, these clarifications comprise such mild changes as

Iam pridem sanus ac ualens id curarat (E479, sig. Y5^v; Leiden edition, I, 815F) with "yes, longe before, in tyme of his helthe" (*The dyaloge called Funus,* p. 41), where the missing verb is implied from the preceding question.

21. *The dyaloge called Funus,* p. 27; E479, sig. X4; Leiden edition, I, 811A.

22. *The dyaloge called Funus,* p. 36; E479, sig. Y2; Leiden edition, I, 814A.

23. *The dyaloge called Funus,* p. 34; E479, sig. Y1; Leiden edition, I, 813D.

24. *The dyaloge called Funus,* pp. 43 and 28; E479, sigs. Y7 and X4^v; Leiden edition, I, 816D and 811C.

specifying indirect objects that are implied in the Latin or inserting speech tags in reported discourse.[25] Elsewhere, the translator adjoins phrases that explain or define. For example, at one place the English text incorporates the greater part of an entry from the Latin *scholia* (appended to some editions, and printed as marginal glosses in others): *Fragmentum plumbi inhaerebat diaphragmati* becomes "A pyece of lead cleued in the skynne, which closeth the herte and the lyghtes about, and dooth seperate them from the mylte and the lyuer, called Diaphragma," where the *scholium* reads, *Diaphragma, est septum transuersum, quod separat praecordia, in quibus cor et pulmo, ab inferiore corporis parte in qua splen, epar et renes.*[26] In other instances, the added material is independent of the Latin text and apparatus. For example, the English text transmits the word *Lethargici* in its Latin form, naturalizing it with a phrase of explanation: "Lethargici that is to say suche as hath the sekenes of forgetfulnesse."[27]

Additions of other sorts range from mere intensifications to moderate embellishments. In an example illustrating the lesser type of change, the meaning contained in the words *Haec aliaque multa fortiter quidem illi detonabant* is only heightened: "These thonderboltes with many other the crossed freres dyde clatter out, and doubtles very manfully."[28] With respect to the practices of other translators in the earlier Tudor period, the embellishments found in this translation are not excessive. Three examples illustrate the limits of the freedom that is taken. When *Grunniebant* becomes "they like hogges grunted," the translation is presenting the greedy actions of the churchmen in the sickroom as more plainly porcine. Similarly, when *mea dedatur orco* reads,

25. For example, *rogabant, ubi uidissent unquam plaustrum quinque rotarum* (E479, sig. X6; Leiden edition, I, 812A) becomes "they asked the fyfth ordre whan euer they dyde se a charyot of .v. wheles" (*The dyaloge called Funus*, p. 30).

26. Compare E479, sigs. Y4 and 2R1ᵛ; Leiden edition, I, 815A–B; and *The dyaloge called Funus*, p. 39. *Scholia* for *Funus* were first printed in the edition of June 1526 (*BB*, E461).

27. E479, sig. X3; Leiden edition, I, 810D; *The dyaloge called Funus*, p. 25.

28. E479, sig. X6; Leiden edition, I, 812B; *The dyaloge called Funus*, p. 30.

"myne I gyue for euer to the derkest pyt of hell," the translation is underscoring the ungodliness attendant upon the Dominican father's offer to forfeit his own soul for that of the sick man. The single reading that comes nearest to being a direct slur on institutions of the Roman Church occurs in an unresisted English pun. Here the translation lingers over *cruciferorum*: "the croked (the crouched freres I wolde say)."[29]

It is likely that the printing of *Funus* in English in 1534 was related to religious and political purposes. But it is difficult to measure that relationship precisely. If not sponsored by the Cromwellian party in government, *The dyaloge called Funus* was nevertheless most probably welcomed by it.[30] The fact that Erasmus attempted in *De utilitate Colloquiorum* to prevent further misinterpretations of *Funus* suggests that even readers on the Continent were ready to take the piece as undermining the authority of the Church. Yet, by translating the greater portion of Erasmus's defense of *Funus* in his introduction, and also paraphrasing that defense as he does, the translator nominally aligns himself with the author in the intended purpose of the work—simply to criticize men, not the institutions within which men err. In the light of King Henry's breach with Rome, however, a book in any way related to the subject of clerical cupidity probably carried political implications that English readers were unlikely to ignore. In this translation, which altered little, it is interesting to note how comfortably Erasmus is appropriated to the spirit—if not the overt work—of the Henrican settlement. The difference between the restrained tone of *The dyaloge*

29. Compare E479, sigs. X7ᵛ, Y2ᵛ, and X6; Leiden edition, I, 812F, 814C, and 812A, with *The dyaloge called Funus*, pp. 32, 37, and 30, respectively.

30. Among recent statements, both specific and general, see A. F. Allison and H. M. Nixon, "Three Sixteenth-Century English Translations of Erasmus in a Contemporary Binding," *British Museum Quarterly*, XXIII (1960–61), 62–63; Thompson, *The Colloquies*, p.359; James Kelsey McConica, *English Humanists and Reformation Politics under Henry VIII and Edward VI* (Oxford, 1965), especially pp. 141–42; E. J. Devereux, "English Translators of Erasmus 1522–1557," in *Editing Sixteenth Century Texts*, ed. R. J. Schoeck (Toronto, 1966), p. 51.

called Funus and the Pope-baiting introduction and interpolating translation of *Epicureus* by Philip Gerrard in 1545 reminds us that the notes of shrill Edwardian Protestantism had not yet sounded in English letters.

There are five later English translations of *Funus*. The 1534 translation had no pronounced influence on readings in any of them. The first of the five was made by William Burton. In "A Popish Funerall," one of *Seven Dialogues both Pithie and Profitable* (1606), Burton attached some breezy, anti-Popish notations to his eclectic, speech-skipping translation. The English into which "H. M., Gent." translated "The Funeral" and all the *Colloquies* (1671) is as literal as the translation of 1534. A carefree idiom and a heady, figurative quality characterize "The Funeral" as "made English"[31] by Sir Roger L'Estrange, in *Twenty Select Colloquies* (1680). "The Funeral," in Nathan Bailey's *Colloquies* (1725), is frequently derivative of readings in both "H. M." and L'Estrange, although the cumulative effect is less rigidly literal than "H. M." and less quixotic than L'Estrange. Professor Thompson's well-accommodated translation of *Funus*, first published in *Ten Colloquies* (1957), now forms part of his complete version of *The Colloquies*. Its English is lively and clear.

DESCRIPTION

Colophon: ¶ At London, by Robert copland, for Io- | han Byddell / otherwyse Salysbu | ry. the .v. daye of Ianuary, | And be for to sell at y̧ sy- | gne of our lady of pyte | nexte to Flete | brydge. | 1.5.3.4.

Collation: 8°. [ ]⁸ B-C⁸ D⁴. [ ]1 wanting. 27 leaves. Repaired slit in [ ]2.

Signatures: $1 signed B-D.

Title signatures: Funus B1, C1; Funus. D1.

Running titles or catchwords: none.

Type: 23 lines. 109 (114) × 74 mm. 95 textura. It is this font of Copland's that Isaac[32] reproduces in fig. 46; *The dyaloge*

31. The phrase is on the title page.

32. Frank Isaac, *English & Scottish Printing Types, 1501–35 * 1508–41,* The Bibliographical Society, Facsimiles and Illustrations, no. II (Oxford, 1930).

called Funus displays the characters that Isaac designates in fig. 1 as s³, v³, w³, y¹, and y². The date at the end of the colophon shows nonranging arabic numerals in what appears to be a smaller font.³³ Copland used three ornamental letters in the book: a Lombardic 'A', of the same size as the text, on B6ᵛ; a block-initial 'M' (18 × 21 mm) on [ ]3ᵛ; an initial 'G' with a grotesque head (21 × 18 mm) on D2ᵛ.³⁴

Copy: British Museum: press mark C. 108. bb. 29 (1).

*References:*³⁵ *STC* 10453.5. Devereux, *A Checklist*, C19.1.

Contents: The missing first leaf may have carried a title page. It may also have disclosed the name of the translator, whose anonymity I cannot remove. Because [ ]2 begins in the midst of a sentence, it is safe to assume that at least [ ]1ᵛ bore some of the preface to the translation. The preface, in which the translator refers to himself in the first person, continues through [ ]3. Half of the surviving text of the preface—that is, from the present beginning on [ ]2 to a point midway through [ ]2ᵛ—is a translation of a portion of Erasmus's specific defense of *Funus* in *De utilitate Colloquiorum*.³⁶ This

---

33. Daniel Berkeley Updike notes the use of "so-called black-letter arabic figures" in *Printing Types, Their History, Forms, and Use*, 2d ed. (Cambridge, Mass., 1937), II, 236.

34. I borrow the term 'Lombardic' from Talbot Baines Reed, *A History of the Old English Letter Foundries* (London, 1887), pp. 88–89, and use it to designate the three styles of 'A' shown by William Blades, *The Biography and Typography of William Caxton* (London, 1877), plate XVII, and the first alphabet shown by Updike, I, fig. 45. See also R. Randolph Karch, *How to Recognize Type Faces* (Bloomington, Ill., 1952), p. 178. Isaac shows capitals other than 'A' in Copland's Lombardic type face in fig. 46, and a de Worde grotesque initial 'W' in fig. 48.

35. Throughout this edition I am grateful to Harvard College Library for information gathered by W. A. Jackson and F. S. Ferguson for the revision of Pollard and Redgrave, *A Short-Title Catalogue*, and to Miss Katharine F. Pantzer, who continues the work. E. J. Devereux, *A Checklist of English Translations of Erasmus to 1700*, Oxford Bibliographical Society, Occasional Publication no. 3 (Oxford, 1968).

36. The translated section, which here ends on p. 21, line 29, corresponds to Leiden edition, I, 906B–C. Matter contained in the opening lines of Erasmus's remarks on *Funus*, which may have preceded the point at which the surviving text of 1534 begins, is here quoted from "The Usefulness of the Colloquies," in Professor Thompson's translation, p. 632: "In *The Funeral*—since death is usually a test of Christian faith—I have portrayed

general defense of the colloquies, appended in Latin editions as a letter to the reader, was initially printed in the second recorded edition to contain *Funus:* the edition printed at Basel in June 1526. In the remainder of the preface, the translator paraphrases what he quotes Erasmus as having intended. The names of the speakers in the dialogue are printed on [ ]3.[37] The dialogue runs from [ ]3ᵛ through D2. D2 also shows an explicit, beneath which is printed the word " ¶Erasmus." and a circular woodcut of the head of Erasmus, 44 mm in diameter. The woodcut that Copland printed here for Byddell appears to be the same cut that Byddell printed for W. Marshall in *A lytle treatise of the maner and forme of confession* (*STC* 10498 [1535?])—another anonymous translation of a work by Erasmus.[38] There is still a third connection between this woodcut and Byddell. It relates to what apparently is a lost edition of the translation printed by Copland. Among books printed by John Skot, Dibdin lists an octavo dated 1534: " 'A necessary and very profytable dyalogue, made by the famous Erasmus, called Funus. Lately traducte into the vulgare tonge, at the request of a certayne gentylman.' With the head of Erasmus in wood."[39] In addition to stating these connections, Professor Devereux has clarified the most likely relationship between these two imprints: because both Copland and Skot printed for de Worde, and because in 1534 de Worde had taken on printing for Byddell, it is probable that the lost edition was printed, like Copland's, for Byddell to publish.[40]

---

in two unsophisticated laymen a contrast in modes of death, placing before your eyes, as though in an actual picture, the different dying of those who put their trust in vanities and those who have fixed . . .' "

37. See the notes below, p. 23.

38. I have seen the woodcut in A4 of the Folger and Harvard copies. It is reproduced in this edition, p. 45.

39. Thomas Frognall Dibdin, *Typographical Antiquities: or the History of Printing in England, Scotland, and Ireland* (London, 1810–19), no. 820. Other bibliographies carry the entry, *e.g.*, William Thomas Lowndes, *The Bibliographer's Manual of English Literature*, ed. Henry G. Bohn (London, 1857–64), p. 750; and *BB*, E837/36.

40. E. J. Devereux, "Some Lost English Translations of Erasmus," *The Library*, 5th ser., XVII, 258. See also Devereux, *A Checklist* (above, n. 35), C19.2.

Filling out part of the final half-sheet, from D2ᵛ through D4, is "A good and a godly admonicion or warnynge, very behouefull for euery chrysten man to loke vpon." A first portion of the "admonicion" declares the debt of thanks that men owe to God. A second portion presents an "Example," which narrates an encounter between the proverbially wise Chanter of Paris and a pious Cistercian shepherd. In their meeting, the simpler man, who weeps joyous tears as he gazes at a toad, expresses gratitude for the divine favor through which God created men in His own image—and not in the ugly likeness of the toad. Although it is not a word-for-word translation, the English version that Copland prints—and possibly may have translated—contains a sufficient number of elements to link it closely with the Latin text of an *exemplum* in *Sermones feriales et communes* of Jacques de Vitry.⁴¹ I have seen versions of the same *exemplum* in four other compilations. These versions—three in Latin and one in Spanish —are apparently repeated from Jacques de Vitry, but they have fewer details in common with the English text that Copland printed.⁴² A third section of the "admonicion" points and amplifies the moral of gratitude that is implicit in the "Example."

Although the first and third parts of the "admonicion" seem merely to introduce and to apply the central "Example," three other possible connections between Copland and the entire "admonicion" occur to me. They are speculations that I cannot rule out.

41. I am grateful to Professor John W. Baldwin for supplying this identification. For modern texts of the *exemplum*, reprinted from Jacques de Vitry, see no. 36 in Joseph Greven, ed., Sammlung mittellateinischer Texte, no. 9 (Heidelberg, 1914), pp. 25–26; no. 35 in Goswin Frenken, ed., *Quellen und Untersuchungen zur lateinischen Philologie des Mittelalters*, Vᴵ (Munich, 1914), 115.

42. The texts I have seen—with their numbers in Frederick R. Goff, *Incunabula in American Libraries, A Third Census* (New York, 1964)—are Johannes de Bromyard, *Summa Praedicantium* ([Basel, not after 1484] = Goff, J 260), G, IV, xx; Johannes Gobius, *Scala Coeli* (Lübeck, 1476; = Goff, G 310), fol. 147; Vincent of Beauvais, *Speculum Morale* (Douay, 1624), column 1550A (for earlier texts see Goff, V 288–291); *El Libro de los Enxemplos*, ed. Pascual de Gayangos, *Biblioteca de Autores Españoles*, LI (Madrid, 1905), 474.

1. Copland may have set type directly from a manuscript or a printed text (now either lost, or extant but unseen by me).
   a. He may have translated a continental text.
   b. He may have printed an English one.
2. Copland may have adapted a manuscript or a printed text that he had once seen, or presently had, in the printing house.
   a. foreign
   b. English
3. Copland, or someone else in the printing house, may have written the entire prose filler, using no written model—although models he did not use may have existed.

In the absence of more facts, and in the knowledge of Copland's frequent writing of preliminary or other additive matter in books that he printed, I leave it as a possibility that Copland translated the *exemplum* from an edition of Jacques de Vitry and padded it with original material of his own to make the complete "admonicion."[43]

D4 also bears the colophon (transcribed above, p. 11). Beneath it is notice of the royal privilege. On D4ᵛ is a printer's device (McKerrow, no. 73).[44] It shows Copland's mark encircled by a garland of roses; beneath the garland is a scroll that bears his name. (Copland is known to have printed at the sign of the Rose Garland in Fleet Street from 1515 to 1535.)[45] In the upper-left corner is a rose on a stem. At upper right the block shows deterioration, but its imprint is less defective than in part i of *A deuout treatyse called the tree & xii. frutes of the holy goost* (STC 13608, 1534). In both books the

43. For comments on Copland's hand in books that he printed, see E. Gordon Duff, *A Century of the English Book Trade* (London, 1905), pp. 31–32; H. S. Bennett, *English Books & Readers, 1475 to 1557* (Cambridge, 1952), p. 163 *et passim*. See also Frank C. Francis, *Robert Copland, Sixteenth-Century Printer and Translator*, Glasgow University Publications, David Murray Foundation Lectures, no. 24 (Glasgow, 1961), pp. 14–15, 22.

44. Ronald B. McKerrow, *Printers' & Publishers' Devices in England & Scotland 1485–1640* (London, 1913; reprinted, 1949). The device is reproduced in this edition, p. 48.

45. Duff, pp. 31–32.

stem of what presumably was a pomegranate remains. (A pomegranate balances a rose in another block that Copland used: McKerrow, no. 71a. Perhaps the pomegranate, because of its relation to the arms of Catherine of Aragon, was cut away.)[46]

Binding: At the time the British Museum acquired it, *The dyaloge called Funus* was sewn with the two other translations now bound with it. The three pieces, however, were stitched together in a different order and lay loose in their covers. Allison and Nixon modestly report the elegant work through which they recognized evidence of an incomplete attempt to enhance the appearance of the volume—that is, to remove the imperfect item from the first place among the three.[47] By observing that mismatched wormholes indicated a recent rearrangement, they established a previous order of binding. As restored to that original order, *The dyaloge called Funus* returned to the first place in the volume. The second is *An epistell of the famous doctor Erasmus of Roterdame vnto . . . Christofer bysshop of Basyle concernyng the forbedynge of eatynge of flesshe* (*STC* 10489.5 [1534?]), printed by Thomas Godfray. The last of the three is *The dialoge betwene Iulius the seconde, Genius, and saynt Peter* (*STC* 14841.5 [1534?]), printed by Robert Copland for John Byddell.

The covers themselves, as Allison and Nixon point out, deserve special mention. The material is contemporary blind-stamped calf. Each cover shows an oblong panel, less tall than wide, for viewing with the fore-edge as its base. Both the side-by-side arrangement on the upper cover, which displays within an interlaced border (56 × 91 mm) the English royal arms at the left of a Tudor rose, and the design on the lower cover, which (in a panel 52 × 89 mm) depicts Saint George slaying the dragon, are apparently unrecorded.

The extent to which all three anonymous translations relate to Erasmus must be qualified. Despite the attractiveness of the association, I know of no piece of scholarship that

46. See Cyril Davenport, *English Heraldic Book-Stamps* (London, 1909), pp. 92–93.

47. *British Museum Quarterly*, XXIII (1960–61), 59.

Upper cover of the volume containing *The dyaloge called Funus*. By permission of the Trustees of the British Museum.

Lower cover of the volume containing *The dyaloge called Funus*. By permission of the Trustees of the British Museum.

proves Erasmus to have been the author of *Iulius exclusus,* from which the third book is translated.[48] Moreover, the arguments of Carl Stange, *Erasmus und Julius II, eine Legende* (Berlin, 1937), cast doubt on existing attributions.

Provenance: No signs reveal the identity of previous owners. As presently rebound, the fresh front paste-down end paper shows only the stamp of the British Museum and the date "Apr 1960"; the verso of the front free end paper shows the volume's press mark: "C 108 bb. 29 | 1–3". Scattered throughout the volume are marginalia in an early hand. Therefore, the only indication of provenance is an external one. Sotheby's catalogue for 29 March 1960 designates the library from which the volume emerged as "The Property of a Lady." Sotheby's could not supply her name. As anticipated by notices printed on the title page of that catalogue, the volume (lot 359) was the central object of attention in the sale.

THE TEXT

The text is set up from the unique copy in the British Museum. Copland's presswork shows twelve abbreviated and contracted forms. I have expanded them silently as follows:

The ampersand to *and*

The tittle above a vowel or consonant to *m* or *n*, as its context requires

The eth-like form ('d' with a stroke through the ascender) to *der*

'p' with a horizontal stroke through the tail to *par* or *per*

'p' with a superior mark to *pre*

'p' with a curly stroke through the tail to *pro*

A terminal, superior loop to *us*

---

48. The printing of the first known edition is [Germany, 1517?]. Its title (from the Harvard copy) is *Iulius. dialogus viri cuiuspiam eruditissimi.* See the description of item no. 27 in the exhibit catalogue, *Erasmus on the 500th anniversary of his birth* (Cambridge, Mass., 1969), compiled by James E. Walsh. J. K. Sowards, who assigns the piece to Erasmus, reviews the scholarship in "Erasmus and the Making of *Julius exclusus*," *Wichita State University Bulletin,* University Studies, no. 60 (Wichita, 1964). See especially n. 13. See also Professor Sowards' introduction to *The Julius exclusus of Erasmus,* tr. P. Pascal (Bloomington, Ind., 1968), pp. 7–23, 97–98.

'v' with a stroke ascending from left to right to *ver*

'w' with superscript 't' to *with*; 'y' with superscript 'e' to *the*; 'y' with superscript 't' to *that*; and 'y' with superscript 'u' to *thou*

Emendation of the copy text is limited to obvious errors. These errors are usually apparent as foul case, literal error, or compositorial repetition. Each emendation is noted at the foot of the page on which it occurs. Certain readings that I declined to emend are also noted. Notes preceded by an asterisk are discussed more fully in the textual notes, appearing below the notes of emendation.

My retention of Copland's punctuation includes his use of the virgule '/' and the question mark that indicates an exclamation. Although the punctuation often reminds us of our distance from sixteenth-century pointing, only where a speech ends in a comma (p. 31, line 32) does it seem to me to jeopardize our understanding of the translator's meaning. In two instances I have emended by adding punctuation at the end of a crowded line in the copy text, where the only apparent reason for its absence was an attempt to justify the line.

Although the type sort 'j' is sometimes used for the terminal 'i' in roman numerals, it does not occur in words. I have followed Copland's use of the letter 'i' for what were in later times distinguished as 'i' and 'j'. His use of initial 'v' and medial 'u' in both lower and upper case is likewise kept. No distinction has been preserved, however, between the normal and round 'r', or the normal and long 's'.

I have followed Copland's use of upper and lower case. The copy text shows no upper case 'w' or 'y'. When expanding abbreviations and contractions, I have also tried to conform to Copland's use of capital letters. Because the text does show 'a' and 't' in upper case, I have, at those places where ampersand, 'y' with superscript 'e', and 'y' with superscript 'u' follow an emphatic stop marked by a period, expanded these abbreviations to *And*, *The*, and *Thou*, respectively. The black letter of the copy text is presented here in roman type.

Introduction

ACKNOWLEDGMENTS

I owe many debts of thanks for help and kindness in preparing this edition. I express particular gratitude to the Trustees of the British Museum for permission to reprint from the copy of *The dyaloge called Funus;* to the University of Illinois for funds in support of several stages of the project; to the staffs of many libraries in Europe and America—particularly to the University of Illinois librarians—for information, books, and microfilms; to friends and colleagues for generous answers to countless questions; to Mrs. Katherine B. Trower, Mrs. Barbara J. Kline, Mr. Daniel P. Poteet, and Mr. James H. De Vries, for their good-natured assistance in work that required much patience. I dedicate this edition to my wife in appreciation of her spirited ability to recite an English or Latin passage from the colloquy upon once overhearing it.

[Translator's Introduction]

theyr hope in the mercy of our lorde, and reprehendynge (as {[ ]2}
it were somwhat in my way) the grete folysshe ambycyon of
ryche men vtteryng theyr superfluyte and arrogancy after
deth, which at the vttermoste, dethe sholde haue fynysshed.
Also I somwhat sharpely rebuke theyr vyce, which for theyr 5
own auauntage, dooth abuse the folyshnesse of ryche men,
whiche they ought specyally to rebuke. For who dare be so
bolde to monysshe lyberally men of grete power and rychesse,
yf suche as professe them deed from the worlde do flatter
theyr vyces / be it there be no suche as I haue dyscrybed, yet 10
notwithstandynge I haue here shewed an example whiche
they ought to eschewe. But and yf there be many thinges
spoken comynly among the people moche more detestable
than these which I haue wryten / than men indifferent may
se therin my cyuylyte, and correct theyr owne vyce. And 15
suche as be not culpable may amend and cause to refrayn
them which dooth other | wyse. Truly I haue spoken noth- {[ ]2ᵛ}
ynge to the reproche of ony state, onelesse ye wyll say, that
he sclaundreth all the chrystianite, which speketh ony thyng
(and that by way of monytion) agaynst the corrupt maners 20
of chrysten men. But it were theyr parte in especyall: whome
the honour of theyr ordre so moche moueth, to restrayne
them whiche with theyr noughty dedes dooth so moche dis-
honest theyr ordre. But in so moche now as they acknowlege
suche theyr faythfull felawes, and moreouer gretely estemeth, 25
and defendeth them. How can they than for shame com-
playne or say that the estymacyon of theyr ordre is ony
thynge empeched of hym that dooth monysshe them for
theyr profyte? Here in I suppose good reder the intent of our
autour, in this sayd dyaloge was to shew rather a loue 30
towarde relygyon and all good relygious men, whiche thing

1 theyr] *the preceding portion of the text is wanting, i.e., leaf* [ ]1.
31 whiche] whithe

caused me the rather to traduct this mater in to our englysshe
{[l3]} tonge / than as some (whose iugementes I do not gre | tely
regarde) sayth that he wryteth agaynst them / ferre dyffer-
yng from the opynyon and mynde of the good relygious fa-
5 ther saynt Hierome, in whose mouthe this saynge was often.
where vice is but generally rebuked there no persone hath
iniury or wronge. whiche lesson after my mynde, were moche
more mete for euery christen man, than vnthankfully to
repyne at suche as be studyous to do them good. Folowynge
10 rather the example of the vnkynd Grekes agaynst theyr good
and valyaunt capytayn Agamemnon, than (as we sholde all)
the chrysten charyte. But I wyll noo lenger hyndre you from
our dyaloge.

[The dyaloge called Funus]

¶ Mercolphus. Phedrus.   Pulcher.|

Mercolphus. Fro whens came hyther Phedrus, suppose ye {[]3ᵛ}
not from Trophonius dene. Phedrus. wherfore doost thou
aske that questyon? Merc. For bycause thou arte moche
sadder than thou arte wonte, more deformed, more fylthy,
more ferse, to make fewe wordes, nothyng at all after thy 5
name. Phed. If (as we se by experyence) they which contynew
ony space in Founders shoppes, draweth to them some
blaknesse. what grete cause hast thou to merueyle, yf I
beyng contynually so many days with two seke men, dyeng
and buryed be more pensyf than I am wont. And also moch 10
the more whan they were bothe my speciall frendes? Merc.
Who doost thou tell me was buryed. Phed. Dydest thou
knowe one George balearyke? Merc. Onely I haue herde of
him. for to my knowlege I neuer sawe his face. Phe. The
other I am sure thou knowest nothynge at all / He was 15
called Cornelius montius, with whome I had | grete famyly- {[]4}
aryte many yeres. Merc. It was neuer my chaunce to be
present at ony mannes dethe. Phed. I haue ben more often
than I wold. Merc. I pray the tell me, is dethe so horryble a
thyng as it is comynly sayd? Phed. The passage toward deth 20
is more harde and paynfull than dethe it self. but he whiche
casteth out of his mynde the ferefulnesse and ymagynacion
of dethe: to hym is released a grete parte of the payne. To

Heading ¶ Mercolphus. Phedrus. *sidenote* Pulcher] ¶ Mercolphus. Phedrus. Pulcher

1 Mercolphus] MErcolphus

Heading ¶ Mercolphus. Phedrus. *sidenote* Pulcher] *Pulcher* was presumably once a parenthetical or a marginal gloss on Lat. *Phaedrus* (φαι-
δρός), with which it is synonymous. It is here moved toward the margin. For
its relation to two editions of a High German translation of *Funus*, see
p. 7 and n. 17, above.

MErcolphius. Fro whens came
hyther Phedrus, Suppose ye
not from Trophonius dene.
Phed?. Wherfore doost thou
aske that questyon? Merc. For bycause þ
arte moche sadder than thou arte wonte,
more deformed, more sylthy, more ferse,
to make fewe wordes, nothyg at all after
thy name. Phed. If(as we se by experyē
ce)they which cōtynewþ ony space in Foū
ders shoppes, draweth to them some blak
nesse. What grete cause hast þ to meruey
le, yf J beyng contynually so many days
with two seke men, dyeng and buryed be
more pensyf than J am wont. ꝯ also moch
the more whan they were bothe my speci
all fredes? Merc. Who doost þ tell me was
buryed. Phed. Dydest þ knowe one Geor
ge balearyke? Merc. Onely J haue herde
of hym. for to my knowlege J neuer sawe
his face. Phc. The other J am sure thou
knowest nothynge at all / He was called
Cornelius montius, with whome J had

Facsimile of sig. [ ]3ᵛ of *The dyaloge called Funus*, with block-initial
'M'. Initial, 18 × 21 mm. By permission of the Trustees of the British
Museum.

speke brefely, all that is paynfull, eyther in sekenesse, or in
dethe, is made more tollerable yf a man commyt hymself
holly to the wyll of god: For as concernyng the felyng of
dethe, (whan the very tyme the soule is departynge from
the body) after my iugement is nothing at all / or (if there 5
be ony) that it is very dull / forbycause nature (before that
come to passe) bryngeth in a slombre, and maketh amased
all the sensyble partyes. Merc. we are all borne without
felyng of our selues. Phed. But not without felyng of our
mother. Merc. why dye we | not in lykewyse? wherfore hath 10{[l4ᵛ}
god appoynted dethe to be so cruciable and paynful a thyng?
Phed. He so ordeyned that our natyuytees sholde be paynfull
and full of peryls to the mother, that she myght so moche
more loue that, whiche she had brought forthe. Contrary
wyse it was his pleasure that dethe sholde be ferefull / leste 15
euery where men shold infere theyr own dethe. For in so
moche that whan we may se dayly many which do slee
themselues, what thynkest thou to come, yf dethe had
nothynge horryble? as often as a man rebuketh his seruaunt
eyther his chylde / yea, as often as the wyfe shold take 20
dyspleasure with her husbande, as often as ony maner of
thing dyde myscary, or ony thing chaunced beyng sorowfull
to the mynde, by and by men wolde renne to hange themselues, to kyll them with swerde, to drawe them to some
conuenyent place where they myght cast themselfes down 25
heedlynges, eyther to poyson / now the bytternesse of dethe
maketh vs that we | loue better our lyfe / in especyal whan {[l5}
physyciens can not heale a man ones deed. Albe it lyke as
we all haue not lyke chaunce in our natyuyte / euen so
there be diuers maners and ways of deth. Some short and 30
swyft deth deliuereth hens. some other wasteth awaye with
slowe dethe. Lethargici that is to say suche as hath the
sekenes of forgetfulnesse. In lykewyse they whiche be stong
of the venymous Aspys altogyder in a slombryng, dyeth
without ony felyng of themselfe. I haue obserued this thyng 35
in especyall, that there is no kynde of dethe so paynful but
it is tollerable after that a man hath with a fully fyxed mynde

3 god:] *impression made by punctuation is indistinct*

decreed for to go hens. Merc. whither of these dethes thynkest thou to be moost lyke the dethe of a chrystyan? Phed. Me semeth the dethe of George more honorable. Merc. But I pray you hath dethe also his couetousnesse of honoure? 5 Phed. I dyde neuer se two persones dyeng so vnlyke a dethe. yf ye haue so moche leysure to here, I wyl shewe you playnly |
{[ ]5ᵛ} the departyng of bothe twayne. but it shall be thy parte to iuge whiche of the dethes is moost to be wysshed to a chrysten man. Merc. yea, mary I pray the that thou wylt 10 not thynke it greuous to tell / for I wolde here nothyng more gladly. Phed. Therfore here first of George. After that deth had shewed certayne and sure tokens of hymself the flocke of phisicions which of longe tyme had take cure of this pacient, nothyng beyng aknowen of the dispayre of lyfe began to aske 15 theyr stypendes. Merc. How many were they? Phed. Somtymes ten, and somtyme twelue, and syx whan they were fewest. Merc. There was ynow to kyl a man in good helthe. Phed. After the tyme they had theyr money / than warned they pryuely suche as were about the seke man, that dethe was at 20 hande. And that they sholde prepayre, and make redy all suche thynges as sholde parteyne vnto the helthe of the soule / seyng that there was no hope at all of ony bodyly welthe.
{[ ]6} And | therupon the seke man was louyngly, by suche as were his special frendes, monysshed that he sholde commyt the 25 cure of his body to god. and that he sholde onely mynde those thynges whiche parteyned to departe wel hens. As soone as George herde these thynges: he loked, and that very very fersly, vpon the physicions / and as it were one sore dyspleased that they shold all gyue hym vp, they sayd to 30 hym agayne, that they were physycions and no goddes / and that they had done so moche as they coude by theyr scyence. albeit that there was no medycyne whiche coude remedy agaynst the ordynaunce of god. This doone, they go in to the next chambre. Merc. what? dyde they tary styl after that 35 they had receyued theyr wages? Phed. They were not yet agreed what kynde of sekenesse it was. One affyrmed that it was a dropsy / another sayd it was a tympany. some sayd it was apostome in the inner partes. some sayd it was one dys-

ease / some another. and all the ty- | me they toke in gouer- {[ ]6ᵛ}
naunce the pacyent they dysputed styfly what maner of
sekenes it shold be. Merc. O, how happy was the pacyent in
the meane tyme? Phed. But bycause at length to ende theyr
contencyon they desyred his wyfe to aske of suche as were 5
his frendes to suffre an Anothomye or section to be made of
the deed body. and that it shold cause moche honour to be
spoken / and also that it was so accustomed to be done for
honours sake in grete noble men. And moreouer that the
thing it self sholde be helthfull to many / and also merytory- 10
ous to the seke man. And the rather to optayn theyr purpose they promised to bye of theyr owne charges a trentall
of masses, for the profyte of the deed. This request hardly,
but at the length with intreatynge of the wyfe and certayn
of his kynsmen was opteyned. These maters doone the garde 15
of physiciens dyde wynde themselues away / for they say
comynly, that it is not conuenyent that they which be wont
to helpe lyfe: | sholde be the beholders of dethe, or be pres- {[ ]7}
ent at buryalles. Anone was called for one Bernardinus a reuerend father as ye knowe well ynough, keper of one of saynt 20
franceys flockes, to here his confessyon. Before the confessyon
was all togyder fynysshed a multytude of the .iiij. ordres,
whome the people call the beggyng ordres was come in to the
hous. Merc. So many deuouring Vultures to one poore pyece
of caryon? Phed. Than afterwarde the parysshe preste was 25
called for to anoyle the man, and to gyue hym the sacrament
of our lordes body. Merc. Deuoutly. Phed. But there was almoost a blody fray betwyxte the parysshe preste and the
other solytary fathers. Merc. At the seke mannes bed? Phed.
And also Chryst hymselfe lokyng vpon them. Merc. what 30
caused all the besynesse so sodeynly? Phed. The parisshe
preste (after that he knewe the seke man was confessed to
the Francyscane) sayd that he wolde neyther mynystre the
sacrament of anoylyng | nor of the aulter / or ony buryeng / {[ ]7ᵛ}
onelesse that he herde with his eares the seke mannes con- 35
fession. He sayd moreouer, that he was the parysshe preste /
and that he must gyue accompt to god for his lytell shepe.
but that he sayd he coude not do yf onely he were ignoraunt

of the secretes of his conscyence. Merc. Semed he not to speke
reasonably? Phed. Not vnto them veryly. For they all cryed
agaynst hym, and in especyall Bernardinus, and Vincentius
the domynycan. Merc. what reasons brought they? Phed.
5 They set vpon the poore preste with grete rebukes and
raylynges / callyng hym often asse, and a mete keper for
hogges. I sayd Vincentius, am a bacheler of dyuynyte formate / and shortly shall be lycencyate / and also shall be
promoted with the tytle of a doctour. Thou arte scarcely
10 come to the redyng of the gospell. How is it than possyble
that thou canst excuse, and iuge the secretes of ony mannes
{[ ]8} conscyence? But and yf thou lyste for to be besyed, | goo see
what thy harlottes, and bastarde brattes doo at home. and
many other obprobryous thynges whiche I am gretly ashamed
15 to shewe. Merc. what sayd he / was he domme at those
wordes? Phed. Domme? yea, thou woldest haue sayd he had
ben as the prouerbe sayth. A greshop taken by the wynges. I
sayd he, shall make of beane stalkes moch better bachelers
than thou arte. The autours and capytaynes of youre ordres
20 Domynyke and Fraunceys, where lerned they I pray you
Aristoteles phylosophy / or the argumentes of Thomas /
eyther Scotus speculacions? or where I pray you were they
made bachelers? ye creped in to the worlde, than easy to beleue your superstycions / but than ye were but a fewe and
25 lowly. and some also meke and wel lerned men. Than your
nestes were in the feldes and poore cotages / but shortly after
ye flitted thens, bothe in to the rychest cytees and in to the
fayrest partes of them. Seyng there be so many poore vyl- |
{[ ]8ᵛ} lages in the countree abrode whiche can not fynde a shepe-
30 herde / there shold ye bestow your labours. there were conuenyent places for you to labour in / but now ye wyll be
nowhere but in the houses of ryche men. ye face and crake
vnder the name of popes / but your pryuyleges be not worth
a strawe: but where as the bysshop, parsone, or vycare dooth
35 not his duety. In my chyrche shall none of you preche so
longe as I am the curate and haue my helthe. I am no bacheler, neyther saynt Martyn was ony bacheler, and yet he

21 phylosophy] phylophy

played the very bysshop. yf I lacke lernyng I wyll not aske it
of you. Suppose ye that the worlde is yet so blynd and folysshe, that (whersoeuer they se saynt Domynyke or Fraunceys cote) they wyll thynke theyr sanctymony and holynes
there to be? or is it to you ony mater at all what I do at home 5
at my hous? what pageauntes ye play in your dennes, and
what knauery ye vse with holy nonnes all the worlde know-
eth. Also how lytell the | better or clener be the ryche mennes [B1]
howses which ye haunt is openly knowen. yea as the prouerbe
sayth, bothe to blere eyed persones and barbours. To tell the 10
what was more spoken I dare not. truly he handled those
reuerend fathers with small reuerence. And none ende sholde
haue ben, oneles Georgius had sygnyfied with waggyng of
his hande, that he wolde say some thyng. Moche adoo it was
to opteyne that theyr chydyng myght cease so longe. than 15
sayd the seke man. Kepe peas betwene you, I wyll confesse
me agayn to the my curate / than after thou shalt be payed
thy money or thou go out of this hous / bothe for bell ryng-
ynge, dyriges, the herse, for buryall vnder stole. neyther by
ony meanes I wyll gyue the occasion to complayn on me. 20
Merc. Dyde the preste refuse so equal a condycion? Phed.
Nothyng at all onely he murmured moche of the confessyon,
which he forgaue the seke man. what nedeth it, sayd he, in
repetyng the same agayn to fatygate and | trouble bothe [B1ᵛ]
the seke man and the preste: in repetyng all one thyng? If 25
he had confessed hym to me in season, parauenture he sholde
haue made his wyll better for his soule helth, now take ye the
charge. This indyfferency of the seke sore agreued those
solytary fathers, nothyng contented that ony morsell of
theyr pray shold be cut out for the parysshe preste. But I 30
went betwene them and concluded so that theyr stryfe was
ended. And the preste anoyled the seke man, and gaue hym
our lordes body. And after he was payde his money and went
his way. Merc. Dyde caulmenes than folowe after so grete a

*34 caulmenes] Caromenes

---

34 caulmenes] Lat. *tranquillitas* (*BB*, E479, sig. X6; Leiden edition,
I, 812A). Among several possibilities, it seems most likely that *Caro-*

tempest? Phed. Nay by saynt Mary, a sharper storme folowed
by and by. Merc. I pray the what was the cause? Phed. Thou
shalt here. There were flocked togyther in one hous foure
ordres of beggyng freres / the fyfthe ordre the whiche be
5 called the croked (the crouched freres I wolde say) came in
[B2] amonge them. Agaynst whiche as it had bene a chylde | base
goten, the other foure arose all togyder makyng no lytell ado.
and they asked the fyfth ordre whan euer they dyde se a
charyot of .v. wheles / or how they durst make mo ordres of
10 beggers than there be Euangelystes. By the same reason
(they sayd) bryng in hyder all beggers whiche vse to syt at
brydges and hye wayes. Merc. what sayd the crouched freres
to that? Phed. They asked the other freres agayn / how the
charyot of the chyrche went, at suche tyme whan there was
15 no ordre of beggers. and agayn whan there was onely one,
and after thre. for truly the nombre (sayd they) of the
euangelystes hath nomore affynyte with our ordres than with
a dyce, which on euery syde shewith .iiij. corners. who
brought the Austyn freres in to the ordre of beggers? or who
20 the Carmelytes? or what tyme begged Augustyn or Hely?
for these they make the auctour of theyr ordres. These thonderboltes with many other the crossed freres dyde clatter out,
[B2ᵛ] and doubtles very man | fully. But bycause they had none
to take parte with them / therfore thynkyng them not able

---

menes is a corruption of *calmenes* or *caulmenes*—despite the fact that *caulmenes* is not recorded as early as 1534. Thomas Cooper's revision of Sir
Thomas Elyot's dictionary, published in 1548, lists *caulmenesse* with three
other meanings for *tranquillitas*. The presence of the printed 'o' is negative
evidence that outweighs the arguments for preserving the reading *Caromenes*. (It is also possible that the 'o' is an 'a' misread from manuscript.)
There are three insufficient reasons for saving the reading. 'C' was often
used as an initial 'c' in secretary hand (see Giles E. Dawson and Laetitia
Kennedy-Skipton, *Elizabethan Handwriting, 1500–1650* [New York, 1966],
p. 13). 'Car' and 'calm' were probably homophones during the period (see
E. J. Dobson, *English Pronunciation, 1500–1700* [Oxford, 1957], II, 992;
Margaret Schlauch, *The English Language in Modern Times* [Warsaw,
1959], p. 90; Henry Cecil Wyld, *A History of Modern Colloquial English*
[Oxford, 1953], pp. 297–99). 'Carom' could be an English borrowing from the
French word *carme*. See *OED, calm*; also, John Palsgrave, *Lesclarcissement
de la Langue Francoyse* ([London] 1530), sig. P4ᵛ, where English *Calme* =
carme.

to resyst the violence of .iiii. suche hostes, gaue place / onely
thretnyng them very cruelly. Merc. Than I trowe there was
nomore brablyng. Phed. No mary. For this parte takynge and
atonement agaynst the fifth ordre was torned in to an open
fray. The francyscan and the domynycan contended, that 5
neyther the augustynyans nor the carmelytes were proprely
called beggers / but rather mungrelles, and chaungelynges.
This stryfe dyde so moche encrease, that playnly I was afrayd
leest it shold come to hand grypes and strokes. Merc. Dyde
the seke man abyde all these brablynges? Phed. These maters 10
were not done at his bed syde, but in a court by whiche ioyned
to the chambre. But all the wordes came to the seke man / for
they dyde not whysper the mater, but it was spoken loude
ynough, and with ful shawmes, as the prouerbe sayth. And
thou knowest moost | comynly that seke men are sharpe of 15 [B3]
heryng in especyally. Merc. But how ended the batayle?
Phed. The seke man sent vnto them his wyfe, to exhorte them
to kepe scylence a lytell whyle, and sayd that he wolde ende
this variaunce. And so desyred, that for that tyme the Augus-
tynyens and the Carmelytes wolde departe / and promised 20
that they sholde lose nothyng therby. And sayd more ouer
that so moche meate sholde be sent home to theyr houses:
as the rest whiche taryed styll sholde haue. But he commaunded that they shold all foure ordres be at his buryeng,
and also the fyfth, and that they shold euery one haue lyke 25
porcion of money. Neuerthelesse he wolde in no wyse that
they shold al syt togyder at dyner, lest ony trouble sholde
insue at theyr metynge. Merc. Thou tellest me of a ryght
good hous keper / whiche at the poynt of dethe coud set in
quyetnes so many besy maters. Phed. He had ben many yeres 30
a capytayn in warres. there are wont dayly to spryng vp
su | che clamoures amonge the souldyours. Merc. was he [B3ᵛ]
ryche? Phed. Very ryche. Merc. But it was euyl goten, with
spoylyng and sacrylege. or robbynge holy places / extorcions
and brybes. Phed. Suche is the comyn facion of the capy- 35
taynes in warres: nor I dare not styfly swere that this man

32 souldyours.] souldyours,

[31]

was altogyder clere and differyng fro theyr maners. But as
ferre as I can perceyue he gate more good with polycy of wyt
than with vyolence. Merc. How so? Phed. He vnderstode
very wel arythmetike or craft of nombryng. Merc. what
5 therof? Phed. what than? To the hygh capytayne he wolde
somtyme accompt .xxx.M. souldyers, whan there were scarcely .vii.M. And more ouer he payd to many of them neuer a
deale. Merc. Certaynly thou shewest me a worthy craft of
accomptyng. Phed. And somtime he caused the warres by
10 craft to contynue and was wont also to receyue euery moneth
money of vyllages and townes: bothe of his enmyes and
[B4] frendes. of his en- | myes: to saue them harmeles, of his frendes
to suffer theym to make peace with theyr ennemyes. Merc.
I knowe of olde the maners of souldyers. but go forthe in your
15 tale. Phed. Bernarde and Vyncent with certayne other of
theyr companyons taryed styll with the seke man / the other
whiche were departed had vytayles sent theym. Merc. Dyde
not they agre well to gyder whiche taryed styll in the house?
Phed. not alway, they like hogges grunted I wote not wher-
20 fore, of the prefermentes of theyr bulles, but leste theyr
deuyse sholde not come to passe, they dissembled for that
tyme. Here they brought forthe his testament, and certayne
demaundes were asked before wytnesses, of suche thynges
whiche they had concluded amonge themselues before. Merc.
25 I am very desyrous to here what thynges they were. Phed. I
shall tell the chyef poyntes, for the mater is somewhat tedy-
ous. There remayned his wyfe .xxxviii. yeres of aege / be-
[B4ᵛ] ynge | a woman certaynly very commendable and wyse. Two
sones, the eldre was .xix. yeres of aege, and the other .xv. And
30 as many doughters, bothe within aege. Thus was it deuysed
by his testament / that his wyfe (bycause they coude not en-
force her to be a Nonne) sholde take the habyte of a Bighyne,
that is an ordre betwene Nonnes and laykes. The elder sone,
bycause they coude not entyse hym to be of ony solitary pro-
35 fessyon. Merc. An olde foxe is taken but seldon in a snare.
Phed. Hastely after his faders burieng they determyned that
he sholde in al haste go to Rome / and there bye the popes
dyspensacyon before his lawful aege to be made a preste, to

syng dayly in Vatycanes temple, for his faders soule. And
that he sholde crepe on his knees euery fryday all the holy
stayres in Laterane. Merc. Dyde he take all this wyllyngly?
Phed. Euen to be playne, as asses be wont to take vpon them
theyr caryages. Moreouer that the yongest sone shold be 5
professed to | saynt Fraunceys, the elder doughter to saynt [B5]
Clare, the yongest to saynt Katheryn. For they coude bryng
nomore of theyr purpose to passe. for George was minded,
bycause he wold haue god more bound to hym, to haue his
wyfe and .iiii. chyldren to be parted amonge the .v. ordres of 10
beggers / and there was grete procurement therto / but the
wife and the eldest sone were to olde to agre thereto, eyther
for fayre wordes or foule. Merc. A propre facyon of dysin-
herytyng. Phed. The inherytaunce altogyder was in suche
wyse deuyded, that after the charges of the buryeng was 15
taken out of all the hole, one parte sholde inure to the wyfe
vpon this condycion / that she sholde lyue with the one halfe
therof / the other half shold be put in the place where she
shold oblyge herself. Fromwhens, yf she at any tyme hereafter
departed, all the same money sholde remayne to that flocke: 20
Another lyke porcion shold be gyuen to the eldest sone, to
whome by and by after sholde be inioyned a iour | ney toward [B5ᵛ]
Rome / and as moche as was suffycient to bye his bulles, and
to paye his costes of meate and drynke at Rome. And yf he
refused to be made preste, his porcion shold than be deuyded 25
betwene the freres of saynt Fraunceys, and of saynt Domynyke / and yet I feare me that he wyll not performe theyr in-
iunction / the yong man appered to abhorre so moche from
holy ordres. Two porcyons sholde be put in to the monastery
which was content to take the yongest sone. Other two partes 30
also to the .ii. monasteryes where the doughters were but vnder this condycion / that yf they at ony tyme hereafter refused
to professe that lyfe, yet all the money sholde be in theyr cus-
tody, sauf, and in no wyse dymynysshed. Agayn on the other
syde, the good father Bernardyne must haue one of the por- 35
cions, and Vyncent another / and half of one of the porcyons

5 Moreouer] More-|uer

to the Charter monkes, for communyon and parte takyng of all good workes, whiche sholde be done in all the ordre. All [B6] the rest | sholde be distrybute to poore people that were pryuely kept / vpon whome Bernardyne and Vyncent thought 5 it best bestowed. Merc. Thou sholdest haue sayd as the lawyers do, Quos vel quas. Phed. After the wyll was redde / they asked him vnder these wordes. George balearike, doost thou beyng on lyue and hole memory approue this testament, which thou lately hast made of thyn own mynde? 10 He answered / I do approue it. And is this thy last and immutable wyl? it is. And thou doost instytute and ordeyn me and fader bacheler Vyncent here: executors of thy last wyll? I do ordeyne. Than they commaunded hym yet ones to subscrybe it with his owne hand. Merc. How coud he, than beyng 15 at poynt of dethe? Phed. Bernardinus dyd gouerne the seke mannes hande. Merc. what dyde he subscrybe? Phed. These wordes. The hygh displeasure of saynt Fraunceys and saynt Domynyke may come to hym whiche gooth about to chaunge ony thing herin. Merc. But feared they not the action called [B6ᵛ]20 in the lawe | Actio inofficiosi testamenti. Phed. No, no: this action lyeth not in those thinges that be dedycate to god / neyther I thynke that ony man is so folysshe to make ony trouble with god. All these maters fynysshed, the wyfe and the chyldren gaue theyr ryght handes to the seke man. swer-25 yng that they shold obserue that thyng whiche they had receyued. ¶ After these thynges they began to comyn (not without stryfe) of the funeral pompe. At last this sentence had the vyctory, that .ix. of euery one of the .v. ordres shold be present in the honour of the .v. bokes of Moyses / and of 30 the .ix. ordres of aungelles. And that euery ordre sholde haue theyr crosse borne before them / and they sholde synge theyr mournyng songes. Moreouer .xxx. (besyde suche as were

*20 inofficiosi] officiosi

28 .ix. of] .ix. of of

20 inofficiosi] Lat. *inofficiosi* (*BB*, E479, sig. Y1; Leiden edition, I, 813D). Unless the translator intended jumbled Latin, *officiosi* collapses the sense of the legal phrase *Actio testamenti inofficiosi.*

kynne to hym) shold be hyred, (for so many pyeces of money
was our lorde solde) all in blacke to bere the torches. And for
his honours sake .xii. mourners. (this nombre is in the honour
of the .xii. apostles,) sholde go about the corps. Next | after [B7]
sholde folowe Georges own hors all in blacke, with his necke 5
so bound doune to his knees as though he wold be sene to
seke his mayster on the erthe. ¶ It was forthermore procured
that the couerynge which shold be cast ouer him, shold shewe
on euery party his armes. Lykewise euery torche and
blacke garment sholde the same. The corps they purposed 10
sholde be layde at the ryght hande of the hygh aulter in a
tombe of marble, whiche sholde be made .iiij. fote hygh fro
the ground. He sholde lye in the top of it grauen in a whyte
marble stone / all armed fro top to toe. neyther myght the
helmet lacke his creste. the creste was the necke of an Ano- 15
crotale. A target in the left arme / in the which was his armes
blased in this wyse, Thre wylde bores heedes all of golde in
a syluer felde. A swerde by his syde with a gylted pomell.
The gyrdle was gylted, and deuyded with studdes of precyous
stones. Golden spurres to his fete, bycause he was a gentyll | 20
man of cote armour, vnder his fete shold be set a leoperd, the [B7ᵛ]
brynkes of his sepulker sholde haue an epitaphye mete for a
worthy man. He was wyllyng that his hert sholde be buried
seuerally in a chapell of saynt franceys. He committed the
other inward partys of his body to the parysshe prest, to be 25
buryed honorably in a chapel of our lady. Merc. An honour-
able buryenge, but very chargeable. At venyce a pore cobler
sholde haue more honour for a lytel coste. for company maketh ornate and elygant the bere, and there somtyme syx hon-
dreth monkes: some in sleueles sloppes, and other some with 30

3 sake .xii.] sake. xii.

4 .xii.] .xii *punctuation wanting at right margin*

12 .iiij.] iiij. *punctuation wanting at left margin*

13 the ground] the the ground

*15–16 Anocrotale] *stet*

15–16 Anocrotale] Lat. *onocrotali*, BB, E479, sig Y1ᵛ; Leiden edition, I,
813F (=pelican). See *onocrotal*, OED.

copes wyll folowe one corps. Phed. I haue sene that myself,
and haue somtime laughed at suche folysshe vaynglories of
poore men. there goeth fullers and curriers before: and coblers
behynd, and monkes in the myddest. thou woldest say they
5 were monsters / neyther here was ony other thynge yf thou
had sene it. It was also prouided by George, that Barnardyne
[B8] and Vyncent shold decerne by lottes | whiche of them sholde
haue the hyghest place in the grete pompe. And afterwarde
other sholde doo soo lykewyse, lest ony rumour or besynesse
10 sholde be for the same. The parysshe preste and his clerkes
were apoynted to the moost inferyour place, that was to go
the formest / neyther the solytary fathers wolde suffre it
otherwyse. Merc. He coude not onely ordeyn an army to
batayle / but also other solempne tryumphes and pompes.
15 Phed. It was also prouyded that the masse of Requiem whiche
sholde be done by the parysshe preste sholde be in prycke
songe, for the more honour. ¶ whyle these thynges and certayne other were in deuysyng, the seke man shaked very sore,
and dyde gyue certayne parfyte tokens that his laste tyme was
20 nygh at hande. The last acte of the comedy was therfore prepared. Merc. Is it not yet at an ende? Phed. The popes bull
was there rehersed / in the whiche was graunted remyssyon of
[B8ᵛ] all his synnes quyte and clene / | and all the feare of purga-
tory was taken away. Beside al these al his goodes was iusty-
25 fied. Merc. Suche as was goten by extorcyon and robbery?
Phed. Certaynly euen suche as were goten by the lawe of
batayle or sowlderye. But it fortuned to be present one
Phylyp a man of lawe the wyfs brother, whiche marked a
place in the bull otherwise set than it ought to be / and
30 caused suspecyon that it was but forged. Merc. Nay, that
was not done in tyme. he sholde haue rather dyssembled it,
though there had ben errour therin / and the seke man sholde
haue done neuer the worse. Phed. I thinke the same. For the
seke man was so troubled with this mater, that he was not
35 ferre of from disperacion. And there father bacheler Vyncent
played the man. He commaunded George to be of a quyet
mynde, he sayd that he had auctoryte bothe to correct ony
thyng whiche was fals in the bulles, eyther to restore ony

thynge that lacketh. But yf the bull deceyue the, euen ve- | ry [C1]
now I put my soule for thyne / that thyne may come to
heuen, and myne I gyue for euer to the derkest pyt of hell.
Merc. But wyll god accept suche chaungyng of soules? and yf
he wolde, was this prouysion for George with suche a guage 5
suffycyent? what and yf the soule of Vyncent was (without
ony chaungyng at all) due to hell. Phed. I shewed you as the
mater was / but Vyncent fynyshed that mater. The pacyent
semed to take a good stomacke to hym / by and by was red
the pardons, wherin was promysed to George to be parte 10
taker of all the workes whiche sholde be done by the .iiii.
ordres, and of the Charter monkes. Mer. I wolde be afrayde
leste I sholde be thurst downe to the botom of hell, yf I sholde
bere suche an vnprofitable burden. Phed. I speke of theyr
good werkes: which dooth no otherwyse aggrauate the soule 15
redy to departe, than fethers dooth the byrde. Merc. To
whome bequeth they theyr yll workes? Phed. To the landes-
kneyghtes | of Germany. Merc. By what auctoryte? Phed. Of [C1ᵛ]
the gospell, sayeng to hym that hath: it shall be gyuen / and
withall was rehersed the nombre of masses and nocturnes, 20
whiche shulde accompanye the dead mannes soule / truely it
was an vnreasonable nombre. After all these thynges, he was
confessed, and had absolucyon. Merc. Dyed he thus? Phed.
Not yet. A matte of russhes was spred vpon the grounde, in
suche wyse that the vpper parte was lapped togyther, for to 25
make as it were a similitude of a bolster. Merc. what ment
they by that? Phed. They sparpled it all ouer with asshes,
but very thynnely, and there they layde the sycke mannes
body. A gray freres cote was spred aboue him, but beyng
halowed before with a certeyn prayers and holy water. A 30
cowle was put vnder his hed, for at that tyme it coulde not be
put vpon hym, and with all was layde the bull and the par-
dons. Merc. A new maner of dethe. Phed. But they af- | fyrme [C2]
styffely that the deuyll hath no power ouer them whiche
dyeth in suche fasshyon. So they sayde that bothe saynt 35
Martyne and saynte Frauncys dyed. Merc. But then theyr
lyues were no lesse vertuous. I praye the tell me what fol-

34 the] he

[37]

owed? Phed. They reachyd the ymage of the crosse, and a
waxe candell to the sycke man. At the syght of the crosse he
sayd, I was wonte in batayles to be defendyd with myne
owne bucklar, but now I wyll put this bucklar agaynste myne
5 enemye, and kyssed it, and put it towarde the left shulder. To
the holy candell he sayd: in tyme past I haue ben valyaunt
in warres with speare, nowe I wyll shake this speare agaynste
the enemy of soules. Merc. Euyn lyke a man of warre. Phed.
These wordes he spake laste / for by and by his tonge was
10 taken with dethe, and with all the pangys of dethe came
vppon hym. Barnardyne stode harde by hym on the ryght
[C2ᵛ] hande, and Vincent on the left syde, bothe | two lowde
ynough / the one shewed the pycture of saynt Franceys, the
other of saynt Domynyke / the other good holy fathers
15 sparpled abrode about the chambre, mombled vp besyly certayn psalmes. Bernardyne with greate out cryes percelled
his ryght eare, and Vyncent the lefte. Merc. what cried they?
Phed. Bernardyne sayd in this wyse. George balearyke, yf
thou now approue those thynges, whiche we haue done be-
20 twyxt vs: bowe downe thy heed towarde thy ryght syde. He
dyde so. Vyncent on the other syde sayd, be nothing adredde
George / thou hast saynt Franceys and saynt Domynyke
thy defenders, care nothing at all. Remembre what a grete
sorte of merytes, what a strong Bull. brefely, remembre that
25 my soule is pledged for thyne, If there were ony ieopardy, yf
thou vnderstand what I say, and also alowest the same, bowe
doun thy heed toward the left syde. He dyde so. And agayn
[C3] with a lyke outcry, they sayd bothe. yf thou thyn | kest sure-
ly all these thynges thyrste downe my hande / and with the

*16 percelled] precelled

---

16 percelled] Lat. *percellebat* (*BB*, E479, sig. Y3ᵛ; Leiden edition, I,
814F), from *percellare* = to strike. *OED* does not record this Latin borrowing. The English prefix is emended to conform to the Latin. Although
it is possible that the translator wrote "pre" or used the manuscript abbreviation for "pre" (the prefixes and their symbols were sometimes used
casually in the sixteenth century; compare Dawson and Kennedy-Skipton,
Elizabethan Handwriting, p. 20, on freedom in the use of "per" and "pro"),
it is more likely that the reading *precelled* is the result of an error in reading
manuscript, in expanding the abbreviation for "per," or in setting type.

same he thirst doune his hande. And so in bowynge his heed
here and there / and puttynge doune handes, was almoost
.iii. houres past. And shortly after whan George began to
gaspe, there Bernardyne standyng vp pronounced the absolucyon / whiche he coude not parfitely fynysshe, before 5
George was departed. this was a lytel after mydnyght. in the
mornyng the Anothomy was made. Merc. what noysome
thyng was founde within him? Phed. Thou remembrest me
in good tyme / for it was gone out of my remembraunce. A
pyece of lead cleued in the skynne, which closeth the herte 10
and the lyghtes about, and dooth seperate them from the
mylte and the lyuer, called Diaphragma. Merc. How came
it there? Ph. His wyfe shewed that he was ones stryken with
a gonne stone / and therof the physyciens coniectured that a
pyece of the lead moltyd, taryed styll within his body. By | 15
and by, the corps all to cut and dilanyate aswell as it wolde [C3ᵛ]
be, was put in a gray freres cote. After dyner, the buryeng
was done with suche and lyke solempnytye, as it was decreed
before. Merc. I neuer herde of a more curious dethe, nor a
corps more ambycyous. But I suppose thou woldest not haue 20
this spoken abroode. Phed. wherefore? Merc. Leste the hur-
nettes wolde be an angred. Phed. There is no ieoperdy at all.
For yf these thynges be godly whiche I shewe, it is theyr
profet that the people do know them / yf they be otherwyse,
so many as be good among them, wyll gyue me thankes 25
whiche haue shewed forthe suche, wherby some correcte with
shame, may refrayne lyke dedes. Also such as be symple, may
take hede lest they be drawen in to like errour / for there be
amonge this sorte great wyse men, and very godly, whiche
hathe often complayned to me, that by the supersticion im- 30
probyte or lewdnes of a fewe, the hole order | is brought to [C4]
hatred of good men. Merc. Thou sayest very ryght, and
boldely / but I am very desyrous to knowe, how Cornelius
dyed. Phed. Like as he lyued greuous to no man, so dyed he.
He was euery yere greued with the febre, commyng to hym 35
at certeyne tymes. The same (bothe for bycause he was some-

what in age: for he was past thre score yeres) or for other
causes more than was wont infebled the man, and it apered
that he felt before that his fatall day was at hande. For the
fourthe daye before he dyed, was Sondaye, our lordes daye,
5 he wente to the temple, was confessyd to his curate, he herde
the commune preachynge and masse / and after the masse
was done, he was howseled, and so wente home. Merc. Vsed
he no Physycyons? Phed. Onely one he counselled, but he
was no lesse a good man, then a good Phisycyon, his name is
10 Iacobus Castrutius. Merc. I knowe hym very well. There is
[C4ᵛ] no more pure man. Phed. | He answered that his frende
sholde not lacke his dylygence / but he thought there was
more socoure in god than in physyciens. Cornelius dyde as
gladly accepte his sayenge, as though he had shewed moost
15 certayne hope of lyfe. Therfore albeit that after his power,
he was always very lyberall towarde the poore, euen than
all that myght be spared from necessary ayde of his wyfe
and chyldren, was dystributed to the poore and nedy men /
and not to the ambycyous beggers, whiche we comynly
20 mete in euery place / but to suche as were to be commended,
whiche fought agaynst pouerte, with al theyr deuyse and
power. I desyred hym to lye hym doune / and rather to call
the preste to hym, than to fatygate with laboure his feble
body. He gaue answere, that his specyall study was euer to
25 helpe his frendes, yf he myght, rather than to put them to
paynes / neyther he wolde be vnlyke to hymself at the tyme
[C5] of his dyenge / neyther truely he laye doune ony | more, but
the last day, and parte of the night, wherin he departed out
of this lyfe. Somtyme for werinesse of his body he walked
30 with a staffe / somtyme reposed in a chayre. He went seldome
to bed, but in his clothes, and his heed reysed vpwarde. All

*1 or] are

---

1 or] Lat. *siue* (*BB*, E479, sig. Y4ᵛ; Leiden edition, I, 815C). I have
emended the reading *are* despite some evidence of a sporadic change in
pronunciation from ŏ to ă in the period. See Karl Luick, *Historische Gram-
matik der englischen Sprache* (Cambridge, Mass., and Stuttgart, 1964), I,
666, and Schlauch, *The English Language*, p. 87.

this tyme he eyther gaue one thing or other to relyue the
poore / but in especyall to them which were knowen poore,
and dwelled nygh to hym, or elles he redde suche thynges in
holy scrypture, whiche prouoketh a mannes conscyence towarde god, and also declareth his charyte towardes vs. And 5
whan he by reason of his werynesse coud not rede hymself,
than he herde some frende redyng before hym. Often tymes
he exhorted with a vehement desyre, his famyly to loue one
another, and to loue the trouthe. He also louyngly conforted
them whiche were pensyfe and sorowfull for his dethe. He 10
gaue often monycion to suche as he put in trust, that nothyng
of his dettes shold be vnpayde. Merc. Made he his wyll? |
Phed. yes, longe before, in tyme of his helthe / for he denayed [C5ᵛ]
vtterly that they were called testamentes, whiche were made
of suche as lye on dyeng: but rather folisshe dotinges. Merc. 15
Dyd he bequethe nothynge to monasteryes, or to nedy men
therin. Phed. Nothyng at all. I (sayd he) haue for my parte
distrybute those lytell goodes whiche god hathe sent me.
Therfore now as I gyue the possession of them to other: so I
gyue also the dispensacyon and orderyng. And I trust that 20
they wyll dyspose them more vertuously, then I haue done
my selfe. Merc. Dyd he not call to him suche holy men
as George dyd. Phed. Neuer one. Neither was there any body
at all with hym, sauyng his owne familie, and two speciall
frendes of his. Merc. I merueyll what he ment. Phed. He said 25
vtterly that he wold be onerous to no mo at his dethe, than
he was at his natiuitie. Merc. I desyre instantly to here the
ende of this mater. Phed. Thou shalt here | it by and by. [C6]
Thursday cam, he laye styll vpon his bed, felynge extreme
werynes of his body / the curate was sent for, and anoyled 30
hym, and by and by gaue hym the body of our lorde, without
any confession at all. For he sayde there was no scrupe and
doubte at all in his mynde, The preste began to aske of hym,
with what pompe, and in what place he wolde be buried. He
sayd agayn, bury me in suche wyse as ye wold bury a christen 35
man of the lowest degree. Nor I care not in what place ye lay
my wretchyd body, whiche shal be founde in the last day aswell out of one place as other, where so euer it be hyd / nor I

regarde any thyng at all the pompe of burieng. Shortly after,
whan mencion was made of the ringyng of belles, trentals,
and yeres myndes, of bulles, of bying part takyng of merites.
Than answered he thus, my curate, I shal do neuer the worse,
5 if no bell at all knoll for me. If it wyll please you to synge one
[C6ᵛ] bare masse for me it shalbe more than nede. | Eyther yf there
be ony thynge elles, whiche (bycause of the comyn custome
of the chyrche) may without offence of suche as be infyrme
persones scarcely be left out, that I permytte to be at your
10 aduyse. Neyther I am minded to bye ony mannes prayers,
eyther to bereue ony man his merytes. Haboundaunce of
merytes floweth ouer in Chryst / and also I trust that the
prayers and merytes of all chrysten men, (yf I be a lyuynge
membre) dooth prouffyte me / Al my hope is in .ii. bulles and
15 pryuyleges / the one is of my offences, that the chyef pastour
Iesus chryst hath clene taken them away, naylyng it to the
crosse. the other is that which he wrote and sealed with his
precyous blode / wherby he put vs in certaynte of euerlasting
lyfe, yf so be that we put all our hole trust in hym. God for-
20 fend that I armed with merytes, and bulles, sholde prouoke
my lorde god, to come in to iugement with his bondman /
[C7] beyng certayne of this: that all which be lyuynge, | shall not
be iustyfied in his syght. I do appele therfore from his iustyce,
to his mercy / for so moche as it is without measure, and in-
25 effable. ¶ After he had spoken these wordes, the preste departed. Cornelius beyng mery and glad (as though he had
conceyued a grete hope of helthe) commaunded that suche
places of holy scrypture sholde be rehersed to hym, as were
wryten to conferme the hope of resurrection, and the rewarde
30 of immortalyte. As for example the texte of Esaye declaryng
the dethe of Ezechias which was deferred, and the cantycle.
Moreouer the .xv. chapytre of the fyrst epystle of Paule to
the Corynthiens. Also out of saynt Iohnn the euangelyst of
the dethe of Lazarus / but namely the history of Chrystes
35 passyon, after the euangelystes. with what a mynde deuoured

14 prouffyte] prousfyte *the* sf *is ligatured*
32 Paule] *the* u *appears to be a broken letter*

he euery thyng. sighyng at some thynges / and whan he herde some other he (lyftyng vp his handes) gaue thankes. At the heryng of dyuers other thynges, he wexed very mery, and | shewed hym outwardly glad / and at many sayenges, [C7ᵛ] he caste out many shorte prayers. After dyner, whan he had 5 taken a lytell slepe, he commaunded that one shulde reherse to hym the .xij. chapytre of saynte Iohnns Gospell, vnto the ende of the history. At whiche tyme thou woldest haue sayde the man had ben clerely transfigured and afflate with a new spirite. Now it drewe to wardes night, he called to hym his 10 wyfe and chyldren. There (his feble body beynge reryd vp as-moche as he coulde suffer) he spake to them in this wyse: Moste dere wyfe, goddes pleasure is nowe to departe them whome he hathe vnyte before / but this separacyon shal be but bodyly, and that for a very shorte tyme. All thy dylygence, 15 loue, and pytye, whiche thou were wont in tyme past to bere toward me and those moste dere chylderen, turne all towardes them. Neyther thynke that thou cannest any wise do higher pleasure to god or me, than yf thou nourysshe, brynge vp, and | instytute theym whiche god hathe gyuen vs twayne, 20 [C8] as fruyte of our maryage: that they may become Chrystes seruauntes. As towardes them therfore double thy loue, and thynke that the porcyon of my loue is translate all in to the / whiche yf thou doest (as I doubte not but thou wylte) they shall in no wyse be sayde Orphanes. But and yf thou doest 25 iterate matrymonye. At that worde the wyfe brast out in wepynge, and began for to swere deuoutely, that she wolde neuer thynke of maryenge agayne. ¶ Here Cornelius sayde. My mooste dere beloued syster in Chryste, yf our lorde Iesus Chryst wyll vouchsafe for to graunte the this purpose, and 30 spyrytuall strengthe, slake not of thy parte from suche an heuenly calling / For that shall be bothe more conuenyent for thyn own self, and also these chyldren. But yf soo be that the infyrmytye, and weykenesse of the flesshe calle the to marye agayne / knowe thou that my dethe | setteth the at lyberte 35 [C8ᵛ] from the lawe of our matrymony / but thou arte not at large

10 to wardes] to | wardes
33 self] felf

[43]

therby from the faythfull promyse, whiche thou hast made in bothe our names: to cure and bryng vp our comyn children. But as touchyng maryage, vse that lyberte whiche god hath permytted the. Onely I pray and put you in remembraunce 5 bothe, that thou do chuse a husbande with suche maners, and thou also vse the towarde hym in suche wyse that he may be led by his mere goodnesse, or prouoked through thy commodite or towardnes to loue his stepe sonnes. Take hede thou doost not bynde thy selfe to ony vowe. Kepe thyselfe at 10 lyberte to god and our chyldren, whome thou must so bryng vp in al mekenesse, that thou be no lesse cyrcumspect / and ware lest they do addyct themselues to ony voluntary purposed lyuyng / vnto the tyme it may appere by theyr aege and dyscrecyon, to what maner of lyuyng they be moost apte.

[Di] 15 ¶ Than after he torned toward his chyldren, and exhor| ted them to the studye of vertue, and obeye theyr moder, and one to loue another. These thynges ended, he kyssed his wyfe, and to his chyldren he gaue his blessyng, makynge ouer them the sygne of the crosse, prayenge god to sende them good 20 mynde, and Christes mercye. After this, he loked vpon all that stode by, and sayde: God that rose agayne in the mornyng, wyll vouchsafe to morow before the sonne ryse, to euocate and call out this symple soule from the sepulchre of this bodye, from the darkenes of this mortalitie, in to his heuenly 25 light. I wyll not that these yong chyldren shall be fatygate and weryed with vayne watchynges. Let all other goo to bedde also / one is suffycyente to watche with me, whome I wolde haue for to reherse some holy scrypture. ¶ whan the nyght was past, a lytell after foure of the clocke, in the pres- 30 ence of all that were in the house, he commaunded one to [Di^v] rede out a lowde the hole psalme whiche our lorde | prayenge, sayde at the tyme he suffered his passyon. That done, he commaunded one to brynge hym an halowed candell, and the sygne of the crucifyxe. He toke the candell in his hande, 35 sayeng, the lorde is my lyghtenynge, and my helthe / whom shall I feare? He also kyssyng the crosse, sayd: The lorde is

17 another] antoher

【44】

protectour, and defender of my lyfe, whom shall I therfore
be adred of? By and by, he helde his handes togyther vpon
his breste, as a man in feruent prayer, lyftyng vp his iyes
towarde heuen, sayd: Lorde Iesu, take my spyryte. And
shortely after, he shytte his iyes, as thoughe he wolde goo to 5
slepe / and therwith, with a softe blast, he yelded vp the
goste. Thou woldest rather haue sayd he had ben on slepe,
than deade. Merc. I neuer herde of dethe more quyet. Phed.
He was of lyke fasshyon in all his lyfe tyme / bothe twayne
were my frendys. Perchaunce I iudge not indyfferently, 10
whether of them departed this lyfe more lyke | a christian. [D2]
Thou Mercolphus, whiche arte not parcyall, shalte more rec-
tely, dyscerne. Merc. So I wyll do, but at a conuenient season.
¶ Finis.

¶ Thus endeth the dyaloge called Funus,   15
made by doctour Erasmus.

¶ Erasmus.

Facsimile of the circular woodcut of the head of Erasmus on sig. D2 of
The dyaloge called Funus. Diameter of original, 44 mm. By permission of
the Trustees of the British Museum.

12–13 rectely] recte-|tely

[D2ᵛ]   ¶ A good and a godly admonicion or warnynge, very behouefull for euery chrysten man to loke vpon.

God hath apparayled the glory of heuen to them that loue
hym, and kepe his commaundementes / and to them that (of
that they haue and done) prayse not them selfe, ne be not
proude therof, and after theyr habilitie departen gladly to
5 the pore and nedy: and set not theyr hertes princypally, but
in our lorde: And to them that the euils, the paines, and the
tribulacions that com to theym, suffren paciently for the loue
of god. And for to haue this great glory, our lorde admonesteth vs that we be alwaye redy, and kepe vs fro synne. And
10 that we put not our hertes principally in this caytyfe worlde,
whiche is nothyng but a lytell passyng, full of wepyng, of
[D3]   sorowes, and of anguisshes, whiche we shall leue. | And take
none hede of the houre without to bere any thyng with vs,
saue the good dedes and the euyll that we haue done. And
15 our body caityfe, shal be couered with the erthe, as a foule
stynkynge carion, and wormes shall eat and wrote therin. Our
lord promyseth not to vs to morow, to thende that our hertes
and our principall intention be in hym, and in his loue. For
we ought to loue god, and to remembre ofte and deuoutly
20 how the swete Iesus vouchedsafe to humble hym selfe for vs,
and descende fro his glory of heuen, in to the wombe of the
glorious virgyn Mary, and becom a man and our brother, and
suffred dethe and passion for vs / and howe he made vs of
nought, and semblable to him / whiche myght haue made vs
25 (yf it had pleased hym) lyke vnto toodes and other wormes.
If we knowe well all the graces that he hath doon to vs, and
thanke and gyue hym laude therfore that is the thyng aboue
[D3ᵛ]   all other, by which we may moost soone and | moost lightely
haue his loue and his grace: moche pleasaunt is it vnto god,
30 whan one knowlegeth the graces and the benefites that he

1 God] GOd

*16 wrote] *stet*

---

16 wrote] var. form of *wroot*, *OED* (=dig)

God hath apparayled the glory
of heuē to them that loue hym,
& kepe his cōmaundementes,
and to them that (of that they
haue & done) prayse not them
selfe, ne be not proude therof, & after theyr
habilitie departen gladly to the pore & nedy: and set not theyr hertes princypally,
but in our lorde: And to them ý the euils,
the paines, and the tribulacions that com
to them, suffren paciently for the loue of
god. And for to haue this great glory, our
lorde admonesteth vs that we be alwaye
redy, and kepe vs fro synne. And that we
put not our hertes principally in this cap
tyfe worlde, whiche is nothyng but a lytell passyng, full of wepyng, of sorowes,
and of anguisshes, whiche we shall leue.

Facsimile of sig. D2ᵛ of *The dyaloge called Funus*, with grotesque 'G'.
Initial, 21 × 18 mm. By permission of the Trustees of the British Museum.

hath done for vs, and whan he is remercyed and thanked therfore.

¶ Example. It is red that the great Chauntre of Paris, founde on a tyme in a felde, a conuerse, (that is to say, a
5 brother, and no preest, of the order of Cisteaulx) kepynge shepe, whiche was contemplatife and deuout towarde god, and wepte ofte in beholdynge a crapaulde or toode. The chauntre demaunded hym wherfore he wepte. He answered to hym, sayenge: I ought well to wepe for my synnes, and
10 gyue thankynges to god, whiche hathe made me to his sem- blaunce. For yf it had pleased hym, he had well made me lyke vnto this crapaulde or toode. Thus this good man thanked and remercyed god. Than let vs rendre and gyue graces and thankynges to our lorde of all his benefites, and
[D4] 15 let vs enioye in hym, and syng we in our | hertes with great ioye / for we be the sones and the doughters of god, made and formed to his semblaunce, bretheren and sisteren of Iesu Christe, and bought and redemed with his preciouse blood, fed with his preciouse bodye, fellowes to aungels of heuen,
20 Coheriters (but yf it be longe of our selfes) for euer more, without ende, of the gloryouse royalme / to the whiche brynge vs the swete and debonayre Iesu Chryste. Amen.

¶ At London, by Robert copland, for Io-
han Byddell / otherwyse Salysbu
25   ry. the .v. daye of Ianuary,
And be for to sell at the sy-
gne of our lady of pyte
nexte to Flete
brydge.

30   1.5.3.4.

¶ Cum priuilegio regali.

[48]

Facsimile of Robert Copland's device (McKerrow, no. 73) on sig. D4ᵛ
of *The dyaloge called Funus*. Original, 95 × 70 mm. By permission of the
Trustees of the British Museum.

The Epicure

Introduction

The first known English translation of Erasmus's colloquy *Epicureus—A very pleasaunt & fruitful Diologe called the Epicure . . . newly translated* by Philip Gerrard (*STC* 10460, 1545)—survives in two copies of one edition, with variant readings. It is only recently that either extant copy of *The Epicure* came into general view. One copy, which was in the library of Sir R. Leicester Harmsworth, was purchased by the Folger Library in 1938 with a large portion of the Harmsworth collection (it is cited hereafter as the *Folger copy*). The Folger copy was thought to be unique until the early 1950's, when a second copy was discovered in Europe. This book—referred to hereafter as the *Harvard copy*—was acquired by Harvard University Library. One purpose in editing *The Epicure* is to make its text as accessible as other early translations of Erasmus's *Colloquies*. Another is to call further attention to a spirited translation that, among its several attractions, exemplifies at once the humanistic reach and the partisan narrowness of literary activity in England during the middle decades of the sixteenth century.

THE TRANSLATOR

Our earliest notice of Philip Gerrard finds him at Court. At the close of the dedicatory letter to Prince Edward in *The Epicure*—printed 29 July 1545, as dated by Grafton's colophon—the translator signed himself "Your humile seruaunt, Philyppe Gerrard, groume of your graces Chambre."[1] It is

1. *The Epicure*, p. 83. The groom of the beds was a servant of the yeoman of the beds, a royal officer in charge of beds (*Middle English Dictionary*, Part B.2, p. 679). Detailed and interesting particulars about these and other offices of the royal household some twenty years earlier are included in "Ordinances for the Household Made at Eltham in the XVIIth Year of King Henry VIII," in *A Collection of Ordinances and Regulations for the Government of the Royal Household, Made in Divers Reigns*, Society of Antiquaries (London, 1790), pp. 139, 149, 151–53, 170, and *passim*. G. Philip

not known when or from what station Gerrard assumed his duties—whether he was part of the initial entourage appointed to care for the newborn Prince at Hampton Court, or a late arrival in Edward's household. The prospect of an advantageous marriage was among the royal favors for which a groom of the bedchamber might hope. Although no record of the marriage itself is found, a letter was written in 1546 (Catherine Parr's fourth year as Henry's Queen) to a "Mrs. Elizabeth Cotton, widow, in the favour of Philip Gerrarde, my lord the Prince his servant, for marriage," at the Queen's Highness' suit.[2]

The year of Henry's death, 1547, marked the publication of Gerrard's book entitled *A Godly Inuectiue in the defence of the Gospell, against such as murmure and woorke what thei can that the Bible shoulde not haue free passage* (*STC* 11797). Whether or not it was in approval of the literary, political, or religious attitudes displayed in *The Epicure*, a promotion to "yeoman of the Chambre"[3] had been conferred upon Gerrard between 1545 and 1547, for it was as such that he signed "The Preface" of the *Inuectiue*.

Like "The Epistle" that accompanied his translation of Erasmus, the *Inuectiue* is a consequence of religious and political commitments that are inseparable. Its "Preface" and "Inuectiue" expand themes, repeat cadences, and borrow phrases from the address to Prince Edward published two years previously. Citing examples to argue that no king, prince, or nation ever prospered that acted against God's word, Gerrard urges King and commons to perceive the plain

---

V. Akrigg, *Jacobean Pageant* (Cambridge, Mass., 1962), p. 25, clarifies the distinction between the Bedchamber and the Privy Chamber, as well as outlining all the offices of the Court in the time of King James I. Lacey Baldwin Smith, *A Tudor Tragedy, The Life and Times of Catherine Howard* (London, 1961), pp. 21–22, also comments on the nature of the offices that Gerrard held.

2. *Letters and Papers, Foreign and Domestic, of the Reign of Henry VIII*, ed. James Gairdner and R. H. Brodie, XXI, part 1 (London, 1908), p. 323.

3. *A Godly Inuectiue* (University Microfilm series, case 8, reel 45), sig. A6ᵛ.

truth of God's intent to see His word spread among all men. Universal familiarity with the English Bible is held a sure deterrent to sedition and other ills of the agitated commonwealth. The godly attainment of one manner and form of worship is pressed as "commodyouse . . . for the weale of this noble realme."⁴ Gerrard discharges animus against all residue of "that foule, stinkyng and Papistycal podel."⁵ This and his tone of rankling aversion express his estimate of the resistance to be overcome in those that "bear lumpyshe heartes toward the truthe"⁶—by which he means the "ignoraunce" of the "dampnable . . . mynisters . . . [who] keepe . . . [the Bible] in staie."⁷

The laudatory notice that Bale, in his *Summarium*, gives to the piety and learning of Gerrard's writings centers, as one would expect, on what opposes the papists.⁸ Bale mentions, also, a sermon in English, which is otherwise unknown: *Inuectiuam in Bibliomastiges, li. I. Affluentia gratiae diuinae prouocer.*

The last of the literary works by which we know Gerrard survives as a manuscript written *ca.* 1552–53: An exhortation to Queen Mary "for the reformation of rentes with yn all . . . [her] realmes and dominions."⁹ The title page, one of two dedications, and the text address King Edward, but evidently the book never reached the reader for whom it was intended. In an inserted dedication to Mary, Gerrard writes of his book, "I gaue it vnto mayster [Sir John] gates then our capten,

4. The same, sigs. D3–D3ᵛ.

5. The same, sig. C5.

6. The same, sig. A5ᵛ.

7. The same, sig. D1.

8. John Bale, *Illustrium maioris Britanniae scriptorum, Summarium* (Ipswich [Wesel], 1548), sigs. 3M4ᵛ–3N1. See the equivalent notice abbreviated in Bale's *Scriptorum Illustrium Catalogus* (Basel, 1557–59), last part, sig. o1ᵛ, and cited by Thomas Tanner, *Bibliotheca Britannico-Hibernica* (London, 1748), p. 312.

9. Cited in the notes hereafter as "Rentes." See *British Museum Catalogue of Western Manuscripts in the Old Royal and King's Collections*, ed. George F. Warner and Julius P. Gilson (London, 1921), II, 233 (MS. Royal 17 B. xl). See also Tanner, *Bibliotheca*, p. 312.

desyrynge hym to delyver it vnto the kynges highnes but after that my capten had read it, he nothynge at all fauerynge the effectes theraf, would not delyver it. but gaue me sore checkes, and streytly charged me to serue yn my callynge and wryte no more vnto his grace."[10] When the passage of time made it possible to submit the treatise again to the throne, there was a new monarch to address. In sending the book to Mary, he appended a plea that the work might be printed.[11] In its final form, addressing each monarch as "defendour of the fayth," the work records a swing of the compass in religious history. As intended for Edward, the author signs himself "your maiesties humble seruant philippe gerrard yeoman of your gard."[12]

In "The Reformation of rentes," Gerrard once again writes to win men's minds. Taking his occasion through the analogy of Christ's asking "his apostels, what opinion the people had yn hym," Gerrard announces, "fit it wer then for your grace to know and aske what your commens saye and thynke by yow."[13] The report gives direct advice: "yf your

10. "Rentes," fol. 2ᵛ. Gerrard's reference to "this last progresse," fol. 8ᵛ, dates the portion of "Rentes" addressed to Edward as after the return of the royal train to Windsor and Hampton Court in mid-September of 1552, upon completion of the King's most venturesome progress. See *Literary Remains of King Edward the Sixth*, ed. John Gough Nichols (London, 1857), pp. cx, cxxxviii, 275, 330, 416, 419, and 436, for details of this and the smaller, interrupted progress of 1551. Gates was appointed Captain of the Guard in April 1551 (see *Dictionary of National Biography*, VII, 942). Gerrard's mention to Mary of having written "a lyttell before" Edward's sickness, fol. 2ᵛ, suggests a date of composition no later than the winter of 1552–53. The King's terminal illness, with specious signs of recovery in May 1553, was noted to have begun in January. See Nichols, pp. clxxvi and cxc.

11. "Rentes," fol. 12ᵛ.

12. "Rentes," fol. 12ᵛ. Perhaps Gerrard's assignment to the Guard preceded the winter of 1548–49. A deposition of that date, giving a list of sums previously disbursed at the King's command (*Literary Remains*, p. cxix), may relate to him: "Item, to Garrat of the gard for a booke [possibly *A Godly Inuectiue* or the sermon Bale mentioned] which he gave the King at St. James .xl. s." It should be noted, however, that other Gerrards were in the King's service.

13. "Rentes," fol. 4ᵛ.

hignes forcast with your self, what thyng hath chefely troden and pulddowen the wealth of england, yow shall playnly fynd, that reasynge of rentes hath brought the greatest part of penurye, and all these our sorowes amongest vs, whych yf your grace pul not dowen shortlyar wyll make your commons worse then slaues."[14] The method of argument is to call to memory the sentence of certain ancient writers[15] on putting "rauen and tyrannie vndrefoote."[16] In urging Edward to do as other kings had done before him, Gerrard laments the fading possibility of England "restored vnto it pristinate wealth and commoditie."[17] He cries out against "those detestable and cruell persons, whom no law could tye, nor shame restreigne, to be content with moderate lyuynges."[18] Edward is enjoined to "cutof theyr monstruous rauen with some open and sharpe punisshement, or els take it awaye by playn statute, whych wer the beneficialst thynge that ever came to england."[19]

Gates's objection to passing the book to Edward may well have been based on Gerrard's implication of laxity on the King's part: "who is ignorant what hath caused your good lawes and statutes to be so lyttell exicuted with yn theyse few yeares? it nedeth not to rehearce what miseries soft aucthoritie hath brought amongest vs of late dayes."[20] Having sought to persuade Edward to take counsel and use strength "to shyttvpp coveteousnes, euen the gate of all wyckednes",[21] Gerrard gives the frail King a stark reminder of "that terrible daye of iudgement . . . whan you shall gyue vpp accompt of this your kyngdome"[22] to God.

14. "Rentes," foll. 8–8ᵛ.

15. "Rentes," fol. 4.

16. "Rentes," fol. 7.

17. "Rentes," fol. 11.

18. "Rentes," fol. 7.

19. "Rentes," fol. 8.

20. "Rentes," fol. 5.

21. "Rentes," fol. 3.

22. "Rentes," foll. 12–12ᵛ.

Introduction

In print or not, Gerrard seems to have succeeded in the service of Philip and Mary. An entry in the *Patent Rolls* dated 24 June 1556 finds him commended for his "service to Henry VIII, Edward VI and the king and queen," and rewarded with a pension,[23] which was renewed by Elizabeth in the first year of her reign.[24] A free grammar school was founded at Hoddesdon, in Hertfordshire, in Elizabeth's second year as Queen, at the suit of Sir Gilbert Gerrard, her Attorney General. On the same occasion she appointed a "Philip Gerard of Hoddesdon [likely the translator of Erasmus whom we have pursued] first and present master of the school for life."[25]

Probability again qualifies the record. Three decades later the very last item of Sir Gilbert Gerrard's will (dated 1592) names a "cousin Phillipe Gerrard" who, if he is the schoolmaster the Attorney General helped to appoint, still may or may not be the translator of *The Epicure*.[26] The Philip Gerrard of *The Epicure* was likely to have been no less than twenty in 1545. Even if he is the legatee of 1592, the past still deprives us. We know little about the translator's passage toward whatever longevity he did attain.[27]

23. *Calendar of the Patent Rolls, Philip and Mary*, III, ed. M. S. Giuseppi (London, 1938), p. 221.

24. *Calendar of the Patent Rolls, Elizabeth*, I, ed. J. H. Collingridge (London, 1939), p. 144.

25. The same, I, 297–98. See also J. A. Tregelles, *A History of Hoddesdon in the County of Hertfordshire* (Hertford, 1908), p. 176.

26. The will is preserved at the Principal Probate Registry, Somerset House (30 Nevill). See also Tregelles, *Hoddesdon*, p. 243.

27. Among other items of possible relation to the translator is a twelfth-century manuscript of the Epistles of Saint Paul in Latin, Saint Jerome's version, bearing the name "philip gerrard" on fol. 1. The name of the owner is written in a sixteenth-century hand. See *British Museum Catalogue of Western Manuscripts in the Old Royal and King's Collections*, I, 79 (MS. Royal 4 A. III).

THE LATIN COLLOQUY
AND THE ENGLISH TRANSLATION

The edition at Basel by Jerome Froben and Nicholas Episcopius in March 1533 was the first to print *Epicureus*.[28] *Problema* and *Epicureus* were the last titles Erasmus added to the *Colloquia*. The collection had grown to include some fifty pieces since the printing of the slim volume of November 1518, which bore the title *Familiarium Colloquiorum Formulae*.[29]

For the twelve years separating the first Latin edition and the printing of Gerrard's *Epicure*, there is record of forty other Latin editions of the complete *Colloquia Familiaria*; six of these are not described in *Bibliotheca Belgica*.[30] In these years there are also three recorded editions of selected colloquies containing *Epicureus*.[31] Hoping to determine which Latin edition Gerrard had before him while making

28. The edition is described in *Bibliotheca Belgica*, ed. F. van der Haeghen, 2d ser., VIII–XI (Ghent, 1891–1923)—hereafter cited as *BB*—no. E483. See also Preserved Smith, *A Key to the Colloquies of Erasmus*, Harvard Theological Studies, XIII (Cambridge, Mass., 1927), pp. 55–56.

29. See P. S. Allen, *Erasmus, Lectures and Wayfaring Sketches* (Oxford, 1934), p. 77. The possibility of arriving at different totals is discussed in Erasmus, *Ten Colloquies*, tr. Craig R. Thompson (New York, 1957), p. xx and n. 19.

30. *BB*, E485–E518. *BB* lists the *Opera Omnia*, printed at Basel by Jerome Froben and Nicholas Episcopius in 1540, in E835/8, but does not describe it. With reference to *BB*, the following numbers may be assigned to the five other editions: [E487^{bis}] to an edition printed at Lyon by Sebastian Gryphius in 1533 (copies in Bibliothèque Nationale and University of Chicago Library); [E496^{bis}] to an edition printed at Antwerp by Johann Grapheus for Johann Steelsius in 1537 (a copy in Bayerische Staatsbibliothek, Munich); [E508^{bis}] to the edition (listed in *BB*, E835/8, but not described) printed at Lyon by Sebastian Gryphius in 1542 (a copy in Yale University Library); [E518^{bis}] and [E518^{ter}] to two editions printed at Antwerp by Johan Critinus (a copy of each in University of Illinois Library). [E518^{ter}] is dated 1545 on the title page. The right half of the title page in [E518^{bis}] is wanting. The two are line-for-line and page-for-page, but they are not the same setting of type. On the basis of a bent, broken border of the ornamental block initial in sig. 2P2 of [E518^{ter}], I am tentatively dating [E518^{bis}] as not after 1545.

31. See *BB*, E484, E692, and E695^{bis}.

his translation, I have examined texts of forty-two of these forty-four recorded editions.[32]

I have not been able to designate one edition as Gerrard's working text. For the following reasons, however, I am able to rule out a total of eighteen editions:[33]

1. E493, E498–E502, E504–E505, E508^{bis}–E509, E511, E514, E517, E518^{bis}, and E518^{ter} omit the words *non canunt* (twenty-seven other texts and Leiden edition, I, 883E), which Gerrard translates "thei sing not" (*The Epicure*, p. 90), from a list of pleasures that some virtuous men forgo.

2. Where the English reads, "the cogname of an Epicure" (*The Epicure*, p. 106), E484 and E692 read, *nomen Epicuri*, instead of *cognomen Epicuri* (forty other texts and Leiden edition, I, 888C).

3. The names of the speakers are reversed throughout the last four-fifths of the dialogue in E492.

4. Where the English reads, "*Ganymedes* the buttler or one lyke vnto hym, standeth euer redye" (*The Epicure*, p. 107), E509 (ruled out in no. 1, above) reads, *adstat pocillator Ganymedes* ∧ *similis* (fol. ccclx^v), not *adstat pocillator Ganymedes aut Ganymedi similis* (forty-one other texts and Leiden edition, I, 888E).

The Italian text, in the translation of the *Colloquia* made by Pietro Lauro Modenese (*BB*, E746; Venice, 1545), has many substantive differences from *The Epicure*. There is no evidence that Gerrard consulted it.

In asking Prince Edward to accept his "rude and simple translation," Philip Gerrard recommended the piece as

32. I have not found copies of two editions described in *BB*. Both locations listed for E488 and all four for E510 report their copies nonexistent, lost, or destroyed.

33. Passages from *Epicureus* in this introduction are quoted from *Des. Erasmi Opera omnia*, ed. J. Clericus (Leiden, 1703–6; reprinted, Hildesheim, 1961–62), hereafter cited as Leiden edition. Occasionally, Leiden edition shows minor differences in spelling from the readings in the sixteenth-century editions. Because these differences do not affect the points being illustrated, no notice is taken of them. My inferior carets indicate where the Latin texts differ.

"very familiar, and one of the godliest Dialoges that any man hath written in the latin tong."[34] Gerrard concluded his preface with the most direct account of his method that he recorded: "There as I doo not folow the latyn, woord for woord, for I omytte that of a certaine set purpose."[35] When the Latin text is read beside the English, Gerrard here seems less to disclaim literal fidelity in translation than to announce his sectarian bias, apparent elsewhere in the preface and in passages interpolated into the text. Gerrard's *Epicure* follows its Latin model with diligence. Not only does it preserve the order of speeches, it retains as a rule Erasmus's sequence of clauses. Except for the translator's freedom with modifiers like adjectives,[36] his dropping a phrase of three Latin words,[37] and twice shortening lists of delights proverbially enjoyed by voluptuaries,[38] all that Erasmus included in the colloquy receives an English counterpart. Thus the English colloquy is more nearly a word-for-word translation than a section-by-section interpretation, best represented in the sixteenth century by North's Plutarch.[39] Yet national idiom and Protestant discipline combine to impart to the piece distinctions of its own.

Lapses from accuracy are infrequent. Little disturbs the sense of the dialogue.[40] One uncertain passage concerns the

34. *The Epicure*, p. 82.

35. The same, p. 83.

36. For example, *elephantem Indicum*, Leiden edition, I, 886A, is translated simply, "the Elephant"; *The Epicure*, p. 99, line 13.

37. *Quid tum postea?* Leiden edition, I, 883C; if translated, it would occur on p. 89, line 30, of *The Epicure*. In *The Colloquies of Erasmus* (Chicago and London, 1965), p. 540, Craig R. Thompson translates the phrase, "What follows?" No Latin edition between 1533 and 1545 that I have examined lacks the passage.

38. Compare Leiden edition, I, 885E, and *The Epicure*, p. 97, line 9, where Gerrard offers no English equivalent for *amores*; compare *phasianis*, I, 888A, and *The Epicure*, p. 104, line 34.

39. For an excellent appreciation of North's method see F. O. Matthiessen, *Translation, an Elizabethan Art* (Cambridge, Mass., 1931), pp. 54–102.

40. Compare Leiden edition, I, 886C, and *The Epicure*, p. 100, where Gerrard stumbles over *sed etiam*.

Ciceronian word *indolentia*, which in its context in *De finibus*[41] —and it is of that context that Erasmus puts us in mind— means a negation of pain, a state of insensibility. Of equal measures of pleasure and pain, Spudeus remarks, *Equidem mallem utroque carere: nam voluptatem emere dolere, non est lucrum, sed pensatio: heic sane potior est ἀναλγησία, quam Cicero ausus est indolentiam appellare.*[42] Gerrard's literal interpretation of *indolentia* imposes an extra burden of moral gravity on Spudeus's speech and, in turn, upon Cicero's wide-ranging dialogue:"Verely I had rather want them booth, for ther is no commoditie nor vantage to bye pleasure with payn but only to chaung one thing for another, but the best choise is nowe not too affectionate anye such leudnes, for *MAR. Tullius* calleth that an inward greife and sorow."[43]

A recurrent liberty that Gerrard takes with Erasmus's *Epicureus* is to enlarge the kernels of Christian morality, with which the colloquy is amply supplied, by the use of synonyms or an added clause. *Ea piis transitus est ad aeternam beatitudinem*, for example, is expanded to "truly that is a right passage for good men vnto all sufficient ioy and perfection accordyng too the iust reward of true religion and vertue."[44]

As well as enlarging the praise of the good, Gerrard casts new scorn on the ungodly, reprimanding them with protracted condemnation. On the remark that creation was

41. See Cicero, *De finibus bonorum et malorum*, tr. H. Rackham, Loeb Classical Library (reprinted, London, 1921), pp. 90, 102.

42. Leiden edition, I, 885B and note.

43. *The Epicure*, p. 95. The Restoration translation by H. M. (1671), p. 532, reads, "which *Cicero* was bold to call *lack of pain*." *The Cambridge Bibliography of English Literature*, ed. F. W. Bateson, II, 32, tentatively identifies H. M. as Henry More or Henry Munday. Nathan Bailey's translation of *The Colloquies*, first printed in 1725, ed. E. Johnson (reprinted, London, 1900), III, 252, reads, "an utter ἀναλγησία, which Cicero calls an Indolency." For an able discussion of Cicero's use of *indolentia* see Edward Surtz, S.J., *The Praise of Pleasure* (Cambridge, Mass., 1960), pp. 13, 31. Walter Kaiser, *Praisers of Folly* (Cambridge, Mass., 1963), pp. 78–81, gives a fine critical appreciation of *Epicureus* and its concept of happiness.

44. *The Epicure*, p. 99; Leiden edition, I, 886A–B.

made for man, Hedonius comments, *Sciunt plerique omnes: sed non omnibus hòc venit in mentem.* Gerrard underscores the censure, "Almoste al knowe that, but some dooe not remembre it," with the interpolated phrase, "shewyng them selues vnthankeful for the great and exhuberant benefittes of god."[45]

Gerrard's tendency to spell out the Christian message is associated, also, with his emphatic commitment to the Bible as the right guide to Christian worship—a commitment that Erasmus had shared without endorsing the same political consequences. Stamping *The Epicure* with the same devotion to the Gospel that he displays in its preface, Gerrard transforms *homines Deo cari* to "such men as the be in fauour of god keping his holy commaundementes and loue his most blessed testament."[46]

One passage calls to mind Gerrard's stated intention to omit "of a certaine set purpose."[47] Here the translator purges his text of several references that might be regarded as indirect compliments to the authority of the Church of Rome. Whereas Erasmus illustrated the spiritual riches of a good conscience by contrasting the inner wealth of a Franciscan with the visible power of temporal rulers, including the pope and his crown, Gerrard reduces the friar to an "honest poore man" and allows the pope to be absorbed in the figure of Sardanapalus.[48]

The full color of Gerrard's bias is applied to the *exemplum* that Hedonius offers about the priest who was versed in magic. When Spudeus interjects, *Eam non didicerat e literis sacris*—"He did not lerne that arte of the holy scripture"[49]— Hedonius replies, *Imo e sacerrimis, hoc est, exsecratissimis.* Letting the pun pass, Gerrard concentrates on the opportunity to abuse the Church of Rome. The slur that Hedonius

45. Leiden edition, I, 887F; *The Epicure*, p. 104.
46. Leiden edition, I, 887D; *The Epicure*, p. 103.
47. *The Epicure*, p. 83.
48. Compare Leiden edition, I, 886B–C, and *The Epicure*, pp. 99–100.
49. Leiden edition, I, 884D; *The Epicure*, p. 93.

is made to speak is worthy of any of the more strident Edwardian pamphleteers: "Yea, rather of most popeholy charmes and witchecraftes: that is too saye, of thinges, cursed, dampnable, and wourthy too bee abhorred."[50] It is in this outburst that Gerrard's translation forces Erasmus nearest to the sustained anti-papal execrations of his own prefatory "Epistle."

Within the swelling periods of Gerrard's preface are a number of vituperative libels. These make the same identifications as his textual interpolations: between deceit, magic, witchcraft, and the "false doctrine"[51] of Roman Catholicism. It is here that Gerrard urges, "it woulde make muche for the weale of this noble realme, yf all men with heart and mynde, would nowe as well expulse the pernitious and deuelyshe doctryne af that Romishe bishop, as his name is blotted in bookes."[52] The figurative half of Gerrard's analogy is in keeping with the turn of events in England. The actual means of suppressing religious and political dissent, which Gerrard foreshadows here, reflect a similarly crude and violent practicality.

DESCRIPTION

Title page: [see facsimile, p. 71, showing McKerrow and Ferguson, no. 54].[53]

Colophon: Imprinted at London vvithin the | precinct of the late dissolued house | of the gray Friers, by Richarde | Grafton, Printer too the | Princes grace. | the. XXIX. | daie of Iuly, the yere | of our Lorde. | M. D. XLV.

Collation: 8°. A–F⁸. Folger copy 47 leaves: F8 wanting. Harvard copy 41 leaves: B1, B8, C8, F4, F5, F7, and F8 wanting.

50. *The Epicure*, p. 93. Bailey (see above, n. 43), III, 250, reads, "From the most unholy ones."

51. *The Epicure*, p. 71.

52. The same, p. 78.

53. See Ronald B. McKerrow and F. S. Ferguson, *Title-page Borders used in England & Scotland 1485–1640* (London, 1932).

Contents: A1 [title]. A1ᵛ *S. Paule to the Ephesians.* [an epigraph summarizing chapters 4–5]. A2–B3 [translator's dedicatory epistle to Prince Edward] *THE HABOVN- | daunt mercie and grace*[.] B3ᵛ–F5ᵛ [the colloquy] The inter-|locutours. [roman] | [bracket] *HEDONIVS | SPVDEVS.* F6 [colophon]. F6ᵛ [block (68 × 49 mm); it is the device of the Prince of Wales, with the initials 'E' and 'P' at the sides of the princely coronet].⁵⁴ F7 [Grafton's device of a grafted tree issuing from a tun. McKerrow, no. 95.⁵⁵ It is seen in books printed in his shop of an earlier and a later date.] F7ᵛ [blank]. F8–8ᵛ [presumably blank].

Signatures: $1–4. A1, B4 unsigned; A5 signed.

Running titles: The Epistle. [black letter] A2ᵛ–B3 (except The Epistle A3, A4, A5ᵛ, A6ᵛ). The Epicure [roman, with a wrong-font italic 'E'] B3ᵛ–F5ᵛ (except four completely roman variants: The Epicure B3ᵛ, C1, C1ᵛ, D1, D8, and E7; The. Epicure, C4, D3ᵛ, E4, and F3; The Epicure. C5, C8, D5, D7ᵛ, E7ᵛ, E8, E8ᵛ, F2, and F5ᵛ; The Epicure, C6ᵛ, D3, E4ᵛ, and F4).

Catchwords: regular except:

A2ᵛ learnyng, | learning   C1 godly | godly.
A5ᵛ sye | sie   C1ᵛ woulde | would
A8ᵛ too | to   C3 wold | would
B2 necli- | necligence,   C3ᵛ ker- | kerdes,
B3 [none]   C4 bee | be
B4ᵛ igno- | ignoraunce   C5 thynges | thinges,
B5ᵛ yng | saiyng.   C7ᵛ done | doone,
B8 ve- | verely   D1ᵛ whiche | which
B8ᵛ *Spe.* | *SPV.*   D2ᵛ lechery | lechery,

---

54. The block is reproduced on p. 110 in this edition. I have seen the same block used in three of Grafton's *Primers: STC* 16034, 16040, and 16042 (all dated 1545). In *STC* 16044 (1546) there is a larger version of the same device. Cyril Davenport, *English Heraldic Book-Stamps* (London, 1909), p. 154, observed that Prince Edward was never invested as Prince of Wales.

55. See Ronald B. McKerrow, *Printers' & Publishers' Devices in England & Scotland 1485–1640* (London, 1913; reprinted, 1949). The device is reproduced in this edition on p. 111.

D4 cience (*low final* 'e' F) |
    cience,
D4ᵛ hym | him HD it F
D7ᵛ ges | ges,
D8 ioye | ioy
D8ᵛ I | (I
E2ᵛ life | lyfe
E3ᵛ nowe | now

E4 sure | sures,
E5 fyndeth | findeth
E7 deyntie | deintye
E8ᵛ reme | then remedy
F2ᵛ peni- | penitent
F4 he | hee
F5 the | ẙ

Type: "The Epistle" 28 lines. 99 (107) × 58 mm. 71 textura. Five various sizes and styles of type are used to set off the ten-line prayer that heads "The Epistle" (sig. A2) and the first line of its text, whose opening is marked by an ornamental block 'W'. Italics ornament the first line of the close of "The Epistle," on B3. The text of *The Epicure* 21 lines.[56] 101 (111) × 58 mm. 96 textura.[57] Roman types are used for the abbreviated names of "The interlocutours"[58] that are prefixed to their speeches. In certain places, roman types also serve to emphasize proper names within the speeches themselves. A different block 'W' marks the start of the dialogue, on B3ᵛ.

References: STC 10460. Devereux, *A Checklist*, C22.[59]

56. There are six exceptions—underset pages with twenty lines: B3ᵛ, B6, C6, D4ᵛ, D6, and D8. Of these only D4ᵛ belongs to the outer forme. The virtual confinement of this irregularity to the inner forme indicates the text of *The Epicure* was cast off and composed by formes. W. H. Bond called attention to the practice in "Casting Off Copy by Elizabethan Printers: A Theory," *Papers of the Bibliographical Society of America*, XLII (1948), 281–91. My inference that *The Epicure* was cast off and set by formes is supported—especially for one sheet—by a unique spelling of one speaker's name throughout the outer forme of sheet B, where every spelling and abbreviation of the name *Spudeus* carries an 'e' in the first syllable: *SPEV.*, *SPE.*, and *Spe*. The inner forme accords with the rest of the dialogue, showing all variants of *SPVDEVS* without this 'e': *SPVDE.*, *SPV.*, and *Spu*.

57. The 96 textura appears to be the type Isaac calls 95 textura. For this and other of Grafton's types see Frank Isaac, *English & Scottish Printing Types 1535–58 * 1552–58* (Oxford, 1932), facsimiles 29–39.

58. *The Epicure*, B3ᵛ (p. 85 of this reprint).

59. E. J. Devereux, *A Checklist of English Translations of Erasmus to 1700*, Oxford Bibliographical Society, Occasional Publication no. 3 (Oxford, 1968).

Binding: Harvard's copy of *The Epicure,* the third item in a worn volume containing four didactic works, is bound in seventeenth-century calf with Baldwin's *Tretise of Morall Phylosophy (STC* 1256, [1555?]), Hales's translation of *The Preceptes of Plutarch for the Preseruacion of Good Healthe (STC* 20062, 1543), and Wilkinson's translation of *The Ethiques of Aristotle (STC* 754, 1547). The Folger copy—its condition excellent—is bound singly in early nineteenth-century calf.

Provenance: Although the known history of ownership of Harvard's copy may be less distinguished than the evident pedigree of the other, it nevertheless supplies information earlier than any we have pertaining to the Folger copy. The Harvard copy was purchased in 1952 from Percy J. Dobell. It appears to have endured sustained abuse from young scholars. The leaves of *The Epicure* and the three works bound with it bear signatures and inscriptions, repeated and elaborated, of Thomas Smith, Robert Palmer of Kington, and "William Asburey his Book an[no] Domin[i] 1689."[60] The inscription "Thomas Hall 1671"[61] and the appearance of the same hand through the volume suggest a date of later limit for the sewing of the four works in one binding.

The notable provenance of the Folger copy includes its purchase, as lot 47 in the Sotheby's sale of 3 April 1856, by a certain "E.S."[62] Bearing a Britwell-Court shelf mark, the collation mark of the bookseller Thomas Thorpe, and the fresh collation of F. S. Ferguson, the copy was listed as lot 191 for

---

60. See especially *The Preceptes,* sig. C3, and *The Epicure,* sig. F6.

61. *The Ethiques of Aristotle,* F1ᵛ, in the Harvard copy.

62. *List of Catalogues of English Book Sales 1676–1900 Now in the British Museum,* ed. Harold Mattingly, I. A. K. Burnett, A. W. Pollard (London, 1915), p. 272. See also *Catalogue of a Valuable Portion of the Library of A Gentleman, Residing in the Country, which will be sold by auction, by Messrs. S. Leigh Sotheby & John Wilkinson, on Thursday, the 3rd of April, 1856* (London, 1856), p. 7. The Harvard University Library's copy of this catalogue is annotated with prices and buyers' names. On this occasion, *The Epicure* brought one pound four shillings.

the Britwell sale, 1 February 1921,[63] but it was privately purchased by Sir R. Leicester Harmsworth in advance of the date on which public auction was to have taken place.[64]

Lost copies: A third copy of *The Epicure*, described by Lowndes and Hazlitt as wanting its title page, and by Hazlitt as having belonged to Dr. Farmer, has presumably fallen from sight.[65] Lowndes's description accords with that of the copy listed as lot 1421 in the White Knights sale of 1819,[66] to which he refers. It was purchased on that occasion for a pound by the bookseller Thomas Rodd.[67]

Two scraps from a copy of *The Epicure* (leaves F6 and F7) are in Printer's Marks, Box 10, of the Constance Meade Collection (Johnson Collection), Oxford.[68] They show no variant features.

THE TEXT

My intention in the present reprint is to reproduce the text of the ideal copy of Gerrard's translation of *The Epicure*. Where the Harvard and Folger copies offer variant readings,

63. See *Catalogue of the Library of S. Christie-Miller, Esq., Britwell, Bucks.* (London, 1873–76), I, 88. See also *Catalogue of Valuable Early English Works on Theology, Divinity, &c. from the renowned library formerly at Britwell Court, Burnham, Bucks* (London, 1921), 2d day (February 1, 1921), p. 24. The lot number is confirmed by *The Britwell Handlist*, comp. Herbert Collmann and G. A. Paternoster Brown (London, 1933), I, 350.

64. Seymour de Ricci, *English Collectors of Books & Manuscripts (1530–1930) and their Marks of Ownership* (reprinted, Bloomington, Ind., 1960), p. 111.

65. William Thomas Lowndes, *The Bibliographer's Manual of English Literature*, ed. Henry G. Bohn (London, 1857–64), p. 750. William Carew Hazlitt, *Second Series of Bibliographical Collections and Notes on Early English Literature, 1474–1700* (London, 1882), p. 205.

66. *White Knights Library, Catalogue of that Distinguished and Celebrated Library* [of George Spencer Churchill, 5th Duke of Marlborough (1766–1840)], *which will be sold by auction by Mr. Evans, June 7, and Eleven following Days* (London, 1819), p. 63.

67. W. A. Jackson kindly let me examine his annotated copy of the *White Knights Catalogue*.

68. I am grateful to Miss Katharine F. Pantzer, Mr. Paul Morgan, and Mr. Harry Carter for information about these leaves.

I have chosen those that show Grafton's text in its corrected state in the pressroom—except where evidence indicates that stop-press alterations depart from what the translator wrote.[69] All variants are recorded in the notes at the foot of the pages on which they occur. They are tabulated by formes, also, on pp. 69–70.

I have emended the copy text where errors originated in the printing house. Such accidents of typography include inverted and dropped letters, readings of type set from foul case, literal errors, and repetitions attributed to a lapse of a compositor's memory. I have emended the punctuation where a comma marks the end of a speech (for example, p. 88:1), and in one instance of double punctuation (p. 98:8). Punctuation is also emended where its absence (for example, from the right margin of a line) seems clearly to be the product of a compositor's effort to justify a crowded line—and then only when that absence endangers the sense of the reading. Similarly, I have emended the use of upper and lower case only when a compositor seems to have selected lower case to save space.

Several of the more important emendations, and some instances in which I have declined to emend, are distinguished by asterisks before the notes that record them; they are discussed in the textual notes, beneath the notes of emendation. I have preserved readings wherein the compositor ran words together—for example, "setfurth" (p. 78:1) and "onesyde" (p. 102:2)—when I found precedent or any other evidence of either the translator's or the printer's intention, but I have spaced out groups of words that seem to have been joined only for the purpose of justifying a line.

Thus, leaving intact an ideal copy of *The Epicure* except for revision of manifest errors, this edition seeks to approximate the readings of a supposed, lost manuscript from which type was set in Grafton's shop. Because the best textual readings—not the dress and trappings—of the edition of 1545 are the object of this reprint, the black letter of the original,

69. See *The Epicure*, pp. 95, 97.

impracticable to reproduce, has been waived in favor of the present roman type. The roman and italic fonts (and swash letters) that ornamented the edition of Grafton are here standardized in *italics*, and distinctions between the sizes of type are ignored.

Further changes of font, as when, for example, the compositor supplements his exhausted stock of black-letter 'Y's with roman and italic capitals, or uses large roman types in the speech headings when all the smaller roman capitals are in type, are not reproduced. Variants of font and punctuation seen in the headlines, discussed above, p. 64, have also been made standard in this edition.

I have followed Grafton's use of the letter 'i' for what were in later times distinguished as 'i' and 'j', and his use of the initial 'v' and medial 'u' in both lower and upper case. No distinction has been preserved, however, between the normal and round 'r' of the black letter or the normal and long 's' of the black letter, roman, and italic types. *The Epicure* employs six contractions, which, along with the ampersand, I have silently expanded as follows:

'y' with a superscript 'e' to *the*, 'y' with a superscript 't' to *that*, 'y' with a superscript 'u' to *thou*, 'w' with a superscript 't' to *with*, 'p' with a curly stroke through the descender to *pro*, and a tittle over a vowel or consonant to *m* or *n*.

Except in transcribing the colophon (p. 63), I have ignored the use of 'vv' for 'w', which occurs only in italics.

SIGLA

F   the Folger copy of *The Epicure*
HD   the Harvard copy of *The Epicure*

PRESS VARIANTS

Sheet B (outer forme)
Corrected: F
Uncorrected: HD

B3 recto.

21–22 la|tyn, woord for woord] la|tyn woord, for woord

B4 verso.

10 can not] cannot

Sheet D (outer forme)

Corrected: F

Uncorrected: HD

D2 verso.

8–9 ple-|sure] plea|sure

D4 verso.

19 crooked,] crooked:

D5 recto.

1 it] him [*catchword on D4 verso* hym]

2 it] he

Sheet D (inner forme)

Corrected: HD

Uncorrected: F

D7 verso.

13 men?] men.

ACKNOWLEDGMENTS

I am pleased to acknowledge the generous help and encouragement that my teachers, Professors W. H. Bond, Herschel Baker, and the late William A. Jackson, gave to me. This edition owes much to their kindly direction. I recall many instances in which they kept me from striking an empty tub.

I am grateful, also, for assistance of various kinds: to the Folger Shakespeare Library and the Harvard University Library for permission to reproduce copies of *The Epicure;* to the Folger Library, again, for granting me a research fellowship enabling me to revise the form that this edition took when I submitted it as a doctoral dissertation; to many libraries in this country and abroad for supplying materials on microfilm; and to the staff of the Widener and Houghton libraries for their sustained help and patience. I wish to record my appreciation of the good cheer and loyalty of my parents by dedicating this edition to them.

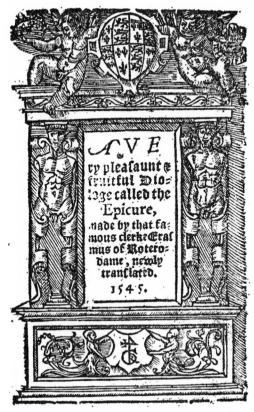

Facsimile of the title page of *The Epicure*. Original, 134 × 83 mm. By permission of the Folger Shakespeare Library.

S. Paule to the Ephesians.

You that haue professed Christ,
suffre not your selues to be decey-
ued with false doctrine, nor vaine
and noughtie talkyng, but herken
vnto all Godly thynges, and
especially too the doctryne
of the Gospell.

[*71*]

THE HABOVN-
daunt mercie and grace of our
heauenly father Iesu Chrift,
maye alwaies ftrengthen
and defende oure noble
& vertuous Prynce Ed-
ward too the mainte-
naunce of the liue-
ly woord of
God.

W HERE
as manye hi-
ftories of olde &
auncient anti-
quitie, and alfo
al godly & Chri-
ftiāwriters moft
playnely confēt
together, and a-
gree in this, that dignitie, riches, kin-
red, wordly pompe, and renoume, doo
neither make men better, ne yet hap-
piat, contrarie too the blynde & fonde
iudgement of the moft part of mennes
but by the power and ftrength of the
mynde, that is, learnyng, wyfedome,
A.ii. and

Facsimile of sig. A2 of *The Epicure*, with block-initial 'W' (initial,
33 × 31 mm). By permission of the Folger Shakespeare Library.

[The Epistle]

THE HABOVN-
daunt mercie and grace of our
heauenly father Iesu Christ,
maye alwaies strengthen
and defende oure noble
and vertuous Prynce Ed-
ward too the mainte-
naunce of the liue-
ly woord of
God.

WHERE as manye histories of olde and auncient antiqui-
tie, and also al godly and Christian writers most playnely
consent together, and agree in this, that dignitie, riches, kin-
red, wordly pompe, and renoume, doo neither make men
better, ne yet happiar, contrarie too the blynde and fonde 5
iudgement of the most part of menne: but by the power and
strength of the mynde, that is, learnyng, wysedome, | and [A2ᵛ]
vertue, all menne are hyghly enriched, ornated, and most
purely beutified, for these bee thinges bothe notable, eternall,
and verye familiar betwene the heauenly father and vs. It is 10
therefore euidente (most excellent Prince) that the fittest
ornamentes for your graces tender age, bee, erudition and
vertue. Wherunto you are bothe so ernestly addicte and
therin so wonderfully doo preuaile, that I nede not too exhorte and exstimulate your grace vnto the study thereof. For 15
that God him self hath wrought, and fourmed your mynde
so apt and desirous too attayne and diligently too seeke for
al godly doctrine, that euen now you doo shewe in all youre

*4 wordly] = *worldly*

---

4 wordly] Compare a similar reading, *wordely,* p. 99, line 2. *OED* records *werdly, wordely,* and *wordlie* among variants of *worldly; word* and
wordle among variants of *world.*

saiynges and dooinges suche a wonderfull pleasauntes much
lyke vnto a certayne swete musike or harmonie, that any honest hart exceadinglye woulde reioyce in the sight therof.
Verely, your grace thinketh plainly all time lost, that is not
5 bestowed vpon learnyng, which is a verie rare thyng in anye
childe, and rarest of all in a Prince. Thus youre noblenes,
[A3] rather desireth vertue and | learning the most surest and ex-
cellent treasures, which farre surmounte all worldly ryches,
then anye vanities or trifles. Nowe youre grace prepareth
10 for the holsome and pleasaunt foode of the mynde. Now you
seke for that whiche you shal fynd most surest helper and
faythfulst councellour in all your affaires. Now your magnifi-
cent mynde studieth that, whiche all Englyshe menne with
meke and humile heartes shuld desire GOD to endue your
15 grace with all. Now with diligent labour you search for a
thyng, as one most myndeful of this saiyng: Happy is that
realme that hath a lerned Prince. Nowe you trauaile for that,
whiche conquereth, and kepeth doune all greuous tourmentes
and outragious affections of the mynde, too the furderaunce
20 of good liuyng, and maintenaunce of vertue, I meane holsome
erudition and learnyng. Many Heathen Princes forsoth, are
highly magnified with most ample prayses, which gaue them
selues too the study of Philosophie, or knowledge of tongues,
[A3ᵛ] for their owne commoditie, and | especially for the weale
25 of their subiectes. Who is nowe more celebrated and worthe-
lier extolled then Mithridates? that noble kyng of Pont and
Bithinia, which, (as Aulus Gellius writeth) vnderstoode so
perfitly the languages of .xxii. sondrye countries that were
vnder his dominion, that he neuer vsed any interpretour too
30 answer his subiectes, but spake their languages so finelye,
as thoughe he had been of the same countrie. Ageyn, that
honorable manne Quintus Ennius saied: that he had .iii.
heartes, because he coulde speake Greke, Italian, and Latin.

*1 pleasauntes] pleasaūtes

---

1 pleasauntes] The spelling is a variant of *pleasance* that is not recorded
in *OED* for the meaning *joy*.

Yea, and breuely, the most famaus writers, as well the Heathen, as the Christien, with an vniuersall consent, playnly
affirme: Whan thei had weied the nature and condicion of
the purest thinges vnder heauen, thei sawe nothyng faire,
or of any pryce, or that ought too be accompted ours, but 5
onely vertue and learning. Euen now too acknowledge that
same, it is yeouen you from aboue, for your grace delecteth
in nothyng more then too bee occupied in the holye Byble:
wherin, | you beginne too sauer and smelle furth the treasure [A4]
of wisedome, knowledge and fulnes of the deuyne power, that 10
is a studie most conuenient for euery Christien Prince, that
kynd of studye cannot haue sufficient laude and commenda-
tion. Whose Princely heart forsoth, is raueshed on suche a
godlie and vertuous studie, it can neuer haue condigne and
worthie praises, but deserueth alwaies too bee had in great 15
price, estimation, and honour. Who dooeth not know? that
Prince which is yeouen vnto the scriptures of God and with
a stoute stomake and valiant heart, both searcheth furth
and also defendeth the true doctrine of the Gospell, too bee
inrolled in the assemble of Christ. Who dooeth not see? that 20
Prince too bee moost surelye armed, which carieth in his
heart the swerd of the spirit, which is the blessed woord of
God. Who is ignoraunt? that euer lastyng lyfe consisteth in
the knoweledge of God. What Prince woulde not studie to
maintaine that, which is written for the health, and saluation 25
of all menne weiynge with himselfe | that a Prince can not [A4ᵛ]
deserue, neither by conquest, ciuel policie, nor yet by anye
other meane vnder heauen, thys name high or honorable, so
wourthely as by the setting forward of Goddes woorde. What
young Prince humily desendyng doune intoo him selfe and 30
callyng to memory his bounden dutie woulde not with a glad
hearte and a chearfull mynde, gredelye desyre too knowe,
enlarge, and amplifie the glory and maiestie of hys derely
beloued father? Your grace (forsoth) hath professed God too
bee your father: Blessed are you then if you obey vn to hys 35
word, and walke in his waies. Blessed are you, yf you sup-

1 famaus] = *var. of* famous *86:3, not in* OED.

porte suche as preache the Gospell. Blessed are you, yf your
mind bee full furnished with the testament of Christ, and
shew your selfe too bee the most cruel foo and enemy agaynst
ypocrisie, supersticion, and all papistical phantasies, wher
5 with the true religion of God hathe been dusked and defaced
these many yeres. Blessed are you, if you reade it daye
and nighte, that your grace maye knowe what GOD dooeth
[A5] forbyd you, and | euer submit your selfe therunto with
seruiceable lowlines chiefly desiring to florysh and decke
10 your mynd with godly knowledge. And most blessed are you,
if you apply your self vnto al good workes, and plant surely
in your heart the scriptures of Christ, If you thus doo, nether
the power of any papistical realme, nor yet of hel can preuaile
at any time against your grace. Nowe therfore, with humile
15 hearte, faithfully receiue the swete promises of the Gospel.
If you kepe the woordes of the Lorde and cleaue fast vnto
them: there is promised you the kingdome of heauen: You
are promised a weale publick most riche and welthy. You are
promised too bee deliuered from the deceiptes of all youre
20 priuie enemyes. You are promised also, too conquere great
and mightie nations. Agayne, let your grace bee most fully
perswaded in this, that ther was neuer Kyng nor Prince, that
prospered whiche tooke parte against Goddes woord, and that
the greatest abhomination that can bee, either for Kyng,
[A5ᵛ]25 Prince, or any other manne, is too for | sake the true woord
of God. O with howe rebukefull woordes and greuous iudgement thei be condemned, which dispice and set lytle by the
holy Byble and most blessed Testament of God, wherin there
is contained all the wil and pleasure of our heauenly father
30 toward vs most miserable and ignoraunt wretches. Who
would not quake, too beholde the terrible feares and threaten-
ynges of God ageinst al suche? Who would not lament and
gladly helppe their obstinate blyndenes? Who woulde not

6 yeres.] yeres
18 welthy.] welthy
28 blessed] bessed
30 wretches.] wretches

weepe? to heare and reade in how many places, they be openly accursed by the scriptures of Christ. God him self playnely
affirmeth, that he wyll sodenly consume them with the breath
of his anger. Yea, besides that whosoeuer declyneth from the
word of God is accursed in all his doynges, whether he be 5
Kyng, or Prynce, riche, or poore, or of what estate soeuer he
bee. This fearfull saiyng (most excellent Prynce) shulde moue
all men to take hede vnto their duties and to praie that gods
word maie take place emongist vs. O that al men would fan-
ta- | sie the scriptures of God, and saye with the vertuous 10[A6]
man Iob. Wee will not bee ageynst the woordes of the holy
one. Truth it is, God taketh diligent care too haue vs al know
his woord. Woulde God therfore, that all wee were now will-
ing to haue the syncere woord of God and all holsom doctrine
too go forward. O that all we would consent togither in the 15
Gospell, brotherly admonishyng, and secretelye prouokyng
one an other too true religion and vertue. O that no man
would sow emongist the people pernitious doctryne, but with
all lowly diligence and Godlye monition euer prouoke, tempt,
and stere them, tyll their heartes were remoued from their 20
olde dautyng dreames and supersticion, which haue been
long grafted in them thorow popyshe doctrine. By this
meane wee shuld euer haue concorde emongist vs, whiche
in all thynges is necessary, but most nedefull and expedient
in Gods holi woord. Now truely the godlyest thynge that can 25
bee deuysed, for any christian realme, is to haue emongist
them one maner and | fourme of doctryne, and too trace [A6ᵛ]
trueli the steppes of God and neuer to seeke any other by-
wayes. Who hath not redde in the scriptures? but that realme
is endued with godly ornamentes and riches, where all men 30
prospere, go forward and florishe in gods woord, delectyng
day and night in the swete consolations of the holy testa-

---

*4 whosoeuer] whoso|euer

---

4 whosoeuer] Compare my emendation, which binds morphemes that
divide over two lines, with the consensus of similar readings: *whosoeuer*,
78:20, 80:20, 85:13; *whersoeuer*, 100:30; *how much soeuer*, 99:30; *what
payne soeuer*, 102:13-14.

ment. By this way we shuld especially setforth the glory of
God, and of our sauiour Iesu Christ, if we would reuerently
shew one an other that whiche God hath taught vs. Yea and
in this doyng all men shulde well perceaue that we were the
5 true disciples of Christ, being knitte and coupled fast together in mynde and iudgement, preachyng God with one
mouth and also with one assent euer promotyng his gloryous
testament. O the good happe and grace of that king or prynce
emongist whose subiectes there is such an hole consent and
10 iudgement in the woord of God, for that most assuredly
byndeth and adiuigneth the hartes of al subiectes too their
kyng. The strength of the Gospell is euen suche in this
[A7] puincte, | that there was neuer man, which did humily re-
ceaue it, that would murmour ageynst his Prince. It teacheth
15 how wyllyngly all men shulde obey their kyng. It sheweth
verye lyuely and most apertly vnto euery man his ful dutie.
It euer prouoketh vs from all wicked, cursed, and most obstinate disobedience. It euer instructeth men too shewe them
selues most lowly, humile, and obesaunt toward their Prynce.
20 Whosoeuer hath tasted fully therof, will declare hym selfe in
al thynges, too bee a faithful subiect. Furthermore, it is clear-
er then the light (most vertuous prince) that it woulde make
muche for the weale of this noble realme, yf all men with
heart and mynde, would nowe as well expulse the pernitious
25 and deuelyshe doctryne af that Romishe bishop, as his name
is blotted in bookes. There is none so ignoraunt, but he knoweth that thorough hym we were brought into a wonderful

*1 setforth] = *set forth*
*11 adiuigneth] = *adjoins*
*25 af] = *of*

---

1 setforth] The run-on is preserved on the basis of similar readings:
The Epicure, 106:26; *Godly Inuectiue*, A2ᵛ, line 3. *OED* lists the form.

11 adiuigneth] A variant of *adjoin*, not listed in *OED* or *MED*, but
compare the variants *adioyne OED* and *adjuggen MED*.

25 af] *OED* lists *af* as obs. var. *of*. Compare a similar reading, *theraf*
[= *therof*], in "Rentes," fol. 2ᵛ, line 18.

blindnes, thorough hym we did sauer of nothyng, but of
stynkyng Ydolatry, through hym we were deceiued with |
false Ypocrisie. Now let euery blind, stiffe hearted, and ob- [A7ᵛ]
stinate creature compare his abhomination with the gospell,
and if he be not shameles, he will abashe to smell of his papis- 5
trie, and to walow still in ignoraunce, vnlest he bee priuely
confederate and in heart consent with the detestable felow-
ship of al wicked papistes. Now would God all suche men
would reduce ageyn their heartes vnto the gospell of Christ.
Would god they would bee prouoked by some meane to desire 10
knowledge. O that god woulde yeoue them a couragious
mynde too reade the gospel, there they shal sone fynde all
the venoume of the romishe sort most playnely detected.
Forsoth wee see dayly, that lacke of knowledge of the gospel
maketh some busserdes runne hedlong on all rockes, daun- 15
gers, and extreme perilles: yea, and beside that, olde popysh
doctryne whiche lyeth folded vp and locked faste in their
heartes, doeth so sore blynd them that they haue neither
fauour ne affection too printe in their myndes, the expressed
councels, admonitions, and | preceptes of the holy scripture, 20[A8]
but too slepe stil in their owne conceites, dreames, and fonde
phansies. Wherfore let your dignitie note well this, that all
those whiche bee not wyllyng that gods woord should bee
knowen, and that blyndenes should be clean expulsed from
all men, whiche be baptised in the blessed bludde of Christ, 25
bewray themselues playne papistes: for in very deede that
most deceatful wolfe and graund maister papist with his
totiens quotiens, and a pena et culpa blesseth all suche as
will bee blynde stil, maintaine his pompe, drinke of his cuppe
of fornication, trust in his pardonnes, liue in popery, ypocri- 30
sie, and damnable ydolatrie, shut vp the kingdome of heauen,
and neuer regarde the gospel. Contrarie too this, christ bi his
holy Prophete calleth al those blessed that seke for his testi-
monies, al those his elect and chosen children, which turne

3 blind,] blind
10 Would] would
20 scripture] scriptnre

[79]

from synne, ypocrisie, and ydolatrie, all those goddes that
heare his word, yea, and breuely, al those which set it forward
honorable men. And in this puincte your grace shoulde euer
[A8ᵛ] beare in mynde, | that noble and vertuous kyng Hezekiah,
5 whiche shewed hymselfe very honorable in setting forward the
woord of God, and therby gotte hym glory and fame immor-
tall, so that nowe he is most highly praysed emongist all men.
Ageyn his subiectes dyd obey his commaundement feynedly
with Ypocrisie, but in their heartes they abhorred gods
10 woord. O the miserie that dyd afterwarde sodeinly ensue vpon
them, O the wonderfull wrath of God that was poured vpon
them, O their great and obstinate blindnes whiche caused
them most greuously too be scourged: Their plage was no
lesse then too bee vtterly spoyled of their enemies, Their
15 plage was no lesse then to eate one an other: Yea, their plage
was no lesse then to eate their owne sonnes and doughters.
This calamitie and sorow (most noble prynce) happened them
because they dyd not regarde the lawes of God, but tourned
too their olde abhominable Ydolatrie, and lightelye estemed
20 gods holy woord. Wherfore euen now whosoeuer is an enemie|
[B1] to the holy Bible, that is, neither studiyng it himselfe, nor
willyng that other men shulde knowe it, he can in no wyse be a
right christian man: although he fast, pray, doo almes, and all
the good workes vnder heauen. And he that hath suche a
25 mynde, is the most cursed and cruel enemie too god, a playne
sower of sedition, and a deuelishe disquieter of all godly men.
For truly those that reade the gospel of Christ, and labour
diligently therin: doo fynde wonderfull rest and quietnes,
from all woofull miserie, perturbation, and vanities of this
30 world. And surely none but ypocrites or els deuilles would go
about too stoppe or allure men from suche a treasure and godly study. And it were conuenient, that all they whiche wyll remayne styll necligent, styffe, and blind: shuld set before
their faces the feare of paynes infernall, and if thei haue any
35 grace at all, their spirites ought to be moued: too note the
great plages that haue happened the slouthful in gods woord,
and those that haue been stubburne ageynst the settyng |

out of it. There bee a thousand recordes and examples in the [B1ᵛ]
holy Bible agaynst such as be farre wyde from knowledge,
and lye now walteryng styl in ignoraunce and will not looke
vpon the bible. It woulde seme, they hope for a thyng, but
their hope is in vaine: For saint Paule plainely writeth the 5
hope of suche ypocrites shall coom too nought. And too conclude (most honorable Prince) seeyng wee haue suche knowledge opened vnto vs, as neuer had englishe men, and are
clearly deliuered from the snares and deceiptes of al false
and wicked doctrine, if we shuld not now thankefully receaue 10
the gospell, and shewe our selues naturally enclyned to set
it forwarde, yea, and pray daye and night vnto God, for the
preseruation and health of the kynges highnes, your graces
deare, and most entierly beloued father, we were neither true
subiectes nor ryght christen men. Forsoth, through the abso- 15
lute wisedome, and the most godly and politike prudencie of
his grace, the swete sounde of gods woorde is gone tho- | rough [B2]
out all this realme, the holye Bible and blessed testament of
oure sauiour Christ are coomne to lighte, and thousandes haue
faithfully receiued those pleasaunt, ioyfull, and most com- 20
fortable promises of God. Surely this thyng before all other,
is acceptable too god. This thyng especially swageth the ire
of god. This thyng in all holi scriptures god most chiefly re-
quireth of his elect and faithfull seruantes, euen too haue his
lytell flocke knowe his blessed woorde, whiche woulde bee 25
muche better knowen and more thankefulli receaued, yf al
agees and degrees of men with one mynd, wyll, and voice,
would nowe drawe after one lyne, leauyng their owne priuate

*6 coom] coom̅
*19 coomne] coom̅ne

---

6 coom] The tittle is nonfunctional. On the casual uses of the tittle,
see Giles E. Dawson and Laetitia Kennedy-Skipton, *Elizabethan Handwriting, 1500–1650* (New York, 1966), pp. 20 and 21.

19 coomne] The tittle in *coom̅ne* is unexpected and presumably nonfunctional. The same participial form as read here, *coomne*, occurs again,
108:30. Another form of the past participle seen in this text is *come*, 85:18.
Compare also *becuñe* [= *becumne*], "Rentes," fol. 2, line 23.

affections, and shewe theim selues euer vigilant, prompt, and
ready helpers and workers with God, (accordynge to the
councell of sainct Paule) and especially priestes, scolemaisters
and parentes, which accordyng too the Prophete Dauid are
5 blessed, if they gladly require the lawe of God. They shuld
therfore reade the bible and purdge theyr mindes of al papist-
[B2ᵛ] ry: for theyr | necligence, in dooyng their duties and slug-
ishnes toward the blessed woord of god, dooeth too muche
appere. Through them forsoth the gospel of Christ shuld bee
10 most strongely warded and defended, for almost all the
Prophetes, and a great parte of the scripture beside teache
them their duties, and shew playnely what maner of men
they shulde bee: Yea, and how greuously the holy Prophetes
crie out vpon false and ignoraunt priestes, the thyng is very
15 euident. But through the helppe of God all those that be ignoraunt, or els learned (as they take them selues) wyll leaue
of, and repent them of their wicked and obstinate blyndnes,
and bowe them selues with all oportunitie too draw mens
heartes too the holy testament of God: consideryng, that in
20 the terrible day of iudgement, euery man shall yeoue ac-
compte of his Beliwicke, where neither ignoraunce shall excuse vs, ne yet any worldly pompe may defend vs. Most
happye then shall they bee, whiche haue walked iustely in the
[B3] sight of the Lorde, and | that haue syncerely preached his
25 testament and lyuely woord withoute flattery or iuggelyng:
Yea, and in that fearful day, all they (as writeth S. Augustine)
shal fynde mercie at the handes of god, whiche haue entised
and allured other vnto goodnes and vertue. Weiyng this with
my self, (most excellent, and vnto all kynd of vertues most
30 prompt and prestant Prince) I thought it good too translate
this Dialoge, called the Epicure, for your grace: whiche semed
too me, too bee very familiar, and one of the godliest Dialoges that any man hath written in the latin tong. Now therfore I most humili praie, that this my rude and simple trans-
35 lation may bee acceptable vnto your grace, trustyng also
that your most approued gentilnes, wil take it in good part.

The Epistle

There as I doo not folow the latyn, woord for woord, for I
omytte that of a certaine set purpose.

    Your humile seruaunt, Philyppe
    Gerrard, groume of your
     graces Chambre.   5

*1 latyn, woord for woord F] latyn woord, for woord HD

---

1 latyn, woord for woord] The relocation of the comma seen in the
Folger copy improves the reading of the Harvard copy; i.e., a stop-press
correction in the outer forme of sheet B.

The Epicure

The inter=
locutours. { *HEDONIVS*
             SPVDEVS.

WHAT meaneth my Spudeus,too applye hys booke ſo er= neſtlye , I pꝛaye you what is the matter you murmour ſo with your ſelfe꞉ SPVDEVS. The truth is (O Hedoni) I ſeke too haue knowlcdge of a thing,but as yet I cannot fynde ẏ whych maketh foꝛ my purpoſe. HEDO What booke haue you there in your boſome꞉ SPVDE . Ciceros dialoge

Facsimile of sig. B3ᵛ of *The Epicure*, with block-initial 'W' (initial, 37 × 35 mm). By permission of the Folger Shakespeare Library.

[The Epicure]

The interlocutours. {*HEDONIVS.*
{*SPVDEVS.*

W*HAT* meaneth mi *Spudeus*, too applye hys booke so er-
nestlye, I praye you what is the matter you murmour so
with your selfe? *SPVDEVS.* The truth is (O *Hedoni*) I seke
too haue knowledge of a thing, but as yet I cannot fynde
that whych maketh for my purpose. *HEDO.* What booke 5
haue you there in your bosome? *SPVDE. Ciceros* | dialoge [B4]
of the endes of goodnes. *HEDO.* It had bene farre more better for you, too haue sought for the begynnynges of godly
thynges, then the endes. *SPVDE.* Yea, but *Marcus Tullius*
nameth that the ende of godlines which is an exquisite, a 10
far passing, and a very absolute goodnes in euerye puincte,
wherein there is contained all kynde of vertu: vnto the knowledge ther of whosoeuer can attaine, shuld desire none other
thing, but hold himselfe hauyng onely that, as one most
fully content and satisfied. *HED.* That is a worke of very 15
great learning and eloquence. But doo you thynke, that you
haue preuailed in any thing there, whereby you haue the ra- |
ther come too the knowledge of the truth? *SPE.* I haue had [B4ᵛ]
such fruite and commoditie by it, that now verelye hereafter
I shall doubt more of the effect and endes of good thinges, 20
then I did before. *HEDO.* It is for husband menne too stande
in doubt how farre the limittes and merebankes extend.
SPE. And I can not but muse styll, yea, and wonder very

Heading HEDONIVS.] HEDONIVS
5 *HEDO.*] HEDO
*17–18 the ra-|ther] = *the more quickly*
*23 can not F] cannot HD

17–18 the ra-|ther] Obs. *OED.* Compare the same reading, *The dya-
loge called Funus*, p. 22:1.

23 can not] Because I accept the Folger reading at 83:1 as a stop-
press correction, I regard *can not* F (over *cannot* HD) at the right

muche, why ther hath been so great controuersie in iudgementes vpon so weightie a matter (as this is) emongist so well
learned menne: especially suche as bee most famous and
auncient writers. *HEDO.* This was euen the cause, where
5 the verite of a thyng is playne and manifest, contrarily, the
[B5] errour through | ignoraunce againe in the same, is soone
great and by diuers meanes encreaseth, for that thei knewe
not the foundation and first beginnyng of the whole matter,
they doo iudge at all auentures and are very fondly dis-
10 ceaued, but whose sentence thynke you too bee truest? *SPE.*
Whan I heare *MARCVS Tullius* reproue the thyng, I then
fantasie none of all their iudgementes, and whan I heare hym
agayne defende the cause: it maketh me more doubtfull then
euer I was and am in suche a studie, that I can say nothyng.
15 But as I suppose the Stoickes haue erred the lest, and nexte
vnto them I commend the *Peripatetickes. HEDO.* Yet I lyke
[B5ᵛ] none of their opini- | ons so well as I doo the Epicures. *SPV.*
And emongist all the sectes: the *Epicures* iudgement is most
reproued and condemned with the whole consent and arbitre-
20 ment of all menne. *HED.* Let vs laye a side all disdayne and
spite of names, and admitte the Epicure too bee suche one,
as euery man maketh of hym. Let vs ponder and weighe the
thyng as it is in very deed. He setteth the high and principall
felicitie of man in pleasure, and thinketh that lyfe most pure
25 and godly, whiche may haue greate delectation and pleasure,
and lytle pensiuenes. *SPV.* It is euen so. *HED.* What more
vertuouser thyng, I praye you, is possible too bee spoken then
[B6] this sai- | yng. *Spu.* Yea, but all menne wonder and crye out
on it, and saye: it is the voyce of a bruite beast, and not of
30 manne. *Hedo.* I knowe thei doo so, but thei erre in the vo-
cables of theise thinges, and are very ignoraunt of the true
and natiue significations of the woordes, for if wee speake of

28 sai- | yng] sai- | saiyng [*catchword* yng]

margin of Grafton's line 10 of B4ᵛ as another stop-press alteration in the
outer forme of sheet B, presumably to justify the line. Compensatory rearrangement of the spacing between words elsewhere within the line (not
shown in this reprint) supports this explanation.

perfecte thynges, no kinde of menne bee more righter *Epi-cures*, then Christen men liuing reuerently towardes God and man, and in the right seruice and worshiping of Christ. *SPV.* But I thinke the *Epicures* bee more nerer and agree rather with the *Cynickes*, then with the Christien sorte: forsoth the 5 Christiens make them selues leane | with fastynge, bewayle [B6ᵛ] and lament their offences, and eyther they bee nowe poore, or elles theyr charitie and liberalitie on the nedye maketh theim poore, thei suffer paciently too bee oppressed of menne that haue great power and take many wronges at their 10 handes, and many men also laughe theim too skorne. Nowe, if pleasure brynge felicitie wyth it, or helpe in anye wyse vnto the furderaunce of vertue: we see playnly that this kynde of lyfe is fardest from al pleasures. *Hedonius.* But doo you not admitte *Plautus* too bee of authoritie? *Speudeus.* 15 Yea, yf he speake vprightely. *Hedonius.* Heare nowe then, and beare awaye wyth you the saiynge of | an vnthriftie [B7] seruaunt, whyche is more wyttier then all the paradoxes of the Stoickes. *SPE.* I tarie to heare what ye wil say. *HEDO.* Ther is nothyng more miserable then a mynd vnquiet and 20 agreued with it selfe. *SPE.* I like this saiyng well, but what doo you gather of it? *HEDO.* If nothing bee more miserable then an vnquiet mynde, it foloweth also, that there is noth-ing happiar, then a mynde voyde of all feare, grudge, and vnquietnes. *SPEV.* Surely you gather the thing together 25 with good reason but that notwithstandynge, in what coun-trie shall you fynde any such mynde, that knoweth not it selfe

3 *SPV.*] *SPV*

4 *Epicures*] *Fpicures*

*16 then] them

19 say.] say

25 vnquietnes.] vnquietnes

---

16 then] Although *them* may be a pronoun whose referent is *the Epicures*, line 4, it is more likely that the translator intended Lat. *Accipe igitur* (Leiden edition, I, 882E) to read, *Heare nowe then*, and that the com-positor misread *thē* from manuscript.

[B7ᵛ] gyltie and culpable in some kynde of euell. *HEDO.* | I call
that euyll, whiche dissolueth the pure loue and amitie betwixt
God and manne. *SPV.* And I suppose there bee verye fewe,
but that thei bee offenders in this thynge. *HEDO.* And in
5 good soth I take it, that al those that bee purdged, are clere:
whych wiped out their fautes with lee of teares, and saltpeter
of sorowfull repentaunce, or els with the fire of charitie, their
offences nowe bee not only smalle grefe and vnquietnes too
them, but also chaunce often for some more godlier purpose,
10 as causing them too lyue afterward more accordyngly vnto
Gods commaundementes. *SPV.* In deede I knowe saltpeter
[B8] and lee, but yet I neuer hearde before, that faultes | haue
been purdged with fire. *H.* Surely, if you go to the minte you
shall see gould fyned wyth fyre, notwithstandyng that ther
15 is also, a certaine kynde of linen that brenneth not if it bee
cast in the fyre, but loketh more whiter then any water
coulde haue made it, and therefore it is called *Linum asbes-*
tinum, a kynde of lynen, whyche canne neither bee quenched
with water nor brent with fyre. *Spu.* Nowe in good faith you
20 bring a paradox more wonderful then all the maruailous and
profound thynges of the Stoickes: lyue thei pleasauntly whom
Chryst calleth blessed for that they mourne and lament?
[B8ᵛ] *Hedonius.* Thei seme too the worlde too mourne, but | verely
they lyue in greate pleasure, and as the commune saiynge is,
25 thei lyue all together in pleasure, in somuche that *SAR-*
DANAPALVS, *Philoxenus*, or *Apitius* compared vnto them:
or anye other spoken of, for the greate desyre and study of
pleasures, did leade but a sorowefull and a myserable lyfe.
Spe. These thinges that you declare bee so straunge and newe,
30 that I can scarcelye yeoue any credite vnto them. *Hedo.*
Proue and assaye them ones, and you shall fynde all my
saiynges so true as the Gospell, and immediatly I shal bryng
the thynge too suche a conclusion (as I suppose) that it shall
[C1] appeare too differ very lytle from the truth. | *SPV.* Make

1 euell.] euell,

21 pleasauntly] pleasa-|sauntly

34 truth. | *SPV*. Make] truth | *SPV.* make

hast then vnto your purpose. *HED.* It shalbe doone if you
wyll graunt me certayne thynges or I begynne. *Spu.* If in
case you demaunde suche as bee resonable. *Hedo.* I wyl take
myne aduauntage, if you confesse the thyng that maketh for
mine intent. *Spu.* Go too. *Hedo.* I thynke ye wyll fyrste 5
graunt me, that ther is great diuersitie betwixt the solle and
the bodye. *Spu.* Euen as much as there is betwene heauen
and yearth, or a thyng earthly and brute, and that whiche
dieth neuer, but alwayes containeth in it the godly nature.
Hedo. And also, that false deceiueable and counterfeited holy 10
thynges, are not too bee taken for those, which in very dede
be | godly. *Spude.* No more then the shaddowes are too bee [C1ᵛ]
estemed for the bodies, or the illusions and wonders of wytch-
craftes or the fantasies of dreames, are too bee taken as true
thynges. *HE.* Hitherto you answer aptly too my purpose, 15
and I thynke you wyl graunt me this thyng also, that true
and godly pleasure can reste and take place no where but
only on such a mynd that is sobree and honest. *SPV.* What
elles? for no man reioyseth too beholde the Sunne, if his eyes
bee bleared or elles delecteth in wyne, if the agew haue in- 20
fected hys tast. *HED.* And the *Epicure* hymselfe, or elles I
am disceiued, would not clippe and enbrace that pleasure,
whiche | would bring with it farre greater payne and suche [C2]
as would bee of long continuaunce. *SPV.* I thynke he woulde
not, if he had any wytte at all. *HED.* Nor you wyll not denye 25
this, that God is the chiefe and especiall goodnes, then whom
there is nothyng fayrer, there is nothyng ameabler, ther is
nothing more delicious and swetter. *SPVDE.* No man wyll
deny thys except he bee very harde hearted and of an vngen-
tler nature then the *Ciclopes. HED.* Nowe you haue graunted 30
vnto me, that none lyue in more pleasure, then thei whyche

6 betwixt] The form *betwxt* also occurs in "Rentes," fol. 7, line 6.

lyue vertuouslye, and agayne, none in more sorowe and
[C2ᵛ] calamytie then those that | lyue vngratiously. *Spu.* Then I
haue graunted more then I thought I had. *He.* But what
thing you haue ones confessed too bee true (as *Plato* sayth)
5 you should not deny it afterward. *SPV.* Go furth with your
matter. *HEDO.* The litle whelpe that is set store and greate
price by, is fed most daintely, lieth soft, plaieth and maketh
pastime continually, doo you thinke that it lyueth plesaunt-
ly? *SPV.* It dooeth truely. *HEDO.* Woulde you wyshe to
10 haue suche a lyfe? *SPV.* God forbyd that, excepte I woulde
rather bee a dogge then a man. *HEDO.* Then you confesse
that all the chief pleasures arise and spring from the mynd,
[C3] as though it were from a welspryng. *SPV.* | That is euident
ynough. *HE.* Forsoth the strength and efficacy of the minde is
15 so great, that often it taketh away the felyng of al externe and
outward pain and maketh that pleasaunt, which by it selfe is
very peynful. *SPV.* We se that dayly in louers, hauyng great
delight to sytte vp long and too daunce attendaunce at their
louers doores all the colde wynter nyghtes. *HEDO.* Now
20 weigh this also, if the naturall loue of man, haue suche great
vehemency in it, which is a commune thyng vnto vs, both
with bulles and dogges, howe much more should all heauenly
loue excell in vs, which commeth of the spirit of Christ, whose
[C3ᵛ] strengthe is of suche power, that it | would make death a
25 thing most terrible, too bee but a pleasure vnto vs. *Spu.*
What other men thinke inwardly I know not, but certes thei
want many pleasures which cleaue fast vnto true and per-
fect vertue. *He.* What pleasures? *Spu.* Thei waxe not rich,
thei optein no promotion, thei banket not, thei daunce not,
30 thei sing not, thei smell not of swete oyntmentes, thei laugh
not, thei play not. *He.* We should haue made no mention in
thys place of ryches and prefermente, for they bryng wyth
them no pleasaunt lyfe, but rather a sadde and a pensiue.
Let vs intreate of other thynges, suche as they chiefely seeke
35 for, whose desyre is to liue deliciously, see ye not daily dron- |

6 *HEDO.] HEDO*
11 man.] man,

The Epicure

kerdes, fooles, and mad menne grinne and leape? *SPV.* I see [C4]
it. *HED.* Do you thynke that thei liue most pleasauntly?
SPV. God send myne enemies such myrth and pleasure. *HE.*
Why so? *Sp.* For ther lacketh emongist them sobrietie of
mind. *HE.* Then you had leuer sit fastyng at your booke, 5
then too make pastime after any suche sorte. *SP.* Of them
both: truly I had rather chose to delue. *H.* For this is plaine
that betwixt the mad man and the drunkerd ther is no
diuersitie, but that slepe wil helpe the one his madnes, and
with much a doo the cure of *Physicions* helpeth the other, 10
but the foole natural diffEreth nothing from a brute beast
except by shape and portrature of body, yet thei | be lesse [C4ᵛ]
miserable whom nature hathe made verye brutes, then those
that walowe theim selues in foule and beastly lustes. *SP.* I
confesse that. *Hedo.* But now tell me, whether you thynke 15
them sobre and wyse, which for playn vanities and shadowes
of plesure, booth dispice the true and godlye pleasures of the
mynde and chose for them selues suche thynges as bee but
vexacion and sorowe. *SPV.* I take it, thei bee not. *Hedo.* In
deede thei bee not drunke with wyne, but with loue, with an- 20
ger, with auarice, with ambicion, and other foule and filthie
desires, whiche kynde of drunkenes is farre worse, then that is
gotten with drinking of wine. Yet *Sirus* that leude compan-
ion | of whom mention is made in the commedie, spake witty [C5]
thynges after he had slepte hym self soobre, and called too 25
memorie his greate and moost beastlye drunkenes: but the
minde that is infected with vicious and noughty desire, hath
muche a doo too call it selfe whom agein? How many yeares

2 it.] it
3 *SPV.*] *SPV*
20 loue,] loue
23–24 companion] cõspaniõ
*28 whom agein?] *question mark punctuates exclamation*

---

28 whom agein?] Compare *scripture?* 93:14. On the use of '?' in ex-
clamatory sentences, see Percy Simpson, *Shakespearian Punctuation* (Oxford, 1911), pp. 85–86; also, Dawson and Kennedy-Skipton, *Elizabethan
Handwriting*, p. 18. *Whom* = home *OED.*

doeth loue, anger, spite, sensualitie, excesse, and ambition, trouble and prouoke the mynde? How many doo wee see, whiche euen from their youth, too their latter dais neuer awake nor repent them of the drunkennes, of ambition, nigard-
5 nes, wanton lust, and riatte? *Spu.* I haue knowen ouermany of that sorte. *Hedo.* You haue graunted that false and fayned
[C5ᵛ] good | thinges, are not too bee estemed for the pure and god-ly. *Sp.* And I affirme that still. *Hedo.* Nor that there is no true and perfect pleasure, except it bee taken of honest and godly
10 thynges. *Spud.* I confesse that. *He.* Then (I pray you) bee not those good that the commune sorte seeke for, they care not howe? *Spu.* I thinke they be not. *Hedo.* Surely if thei were good, they would not chaunce but onely too good men: and would make all those vertuous that they happen vntoo.
15 What maner of pleasure make you that, doo you thinke it too bee godly, which is not of true and honest thynges, but of deceatfull: and coometh out of the shadowes of good thynges?
[C6] *Sp.* | Nay in noo wyse. *He.* For pleasure maketh vs to liue merely. *Spu.* Yea, nothyng so muche. *He.* Therfore no man
20 truely liueth pleasauntly, but he that lyueth godly: that is, whiche vseth and delecteth onli in good thynges: for vertue of it selfe, maketh a man to habound in all thynges that bee good, perfete, and prayse worthy: yea, it onely prouoketh God the fountaine of all goodnes, too loue and fauour man.
25 *SP.* I almost consent with you. *HED.* But now marke howe far they bee from all pleasure, whiche seeme openly emongist all men too folowe nothyng, but an inordinate de-
[C6ᵛ] lectation in thynges carnall. | First their mynde is vile, and corrupted with the sauour and taste of noughtie desires, in
30 so muche that if any pleasaunt thing chaunce them, forth-with it waxeth bitter, and is nought set by, in like maner as where the welle hed is corrupted and stynketh, there the water must nedes be vnsauery. Agein ther is no honest pleasure, but that whiche wee receaue with a sobre and a
35 quiet mynde. For wee see, nothyng reioyseth the angry man more, then too bee reuenged on his offenders, but that plea-

28 in] in | in

sure is turned into pain after his rage bee past, and anger subdued. *Spu.* I say not the contrary. *He.* Finally, suche leude pleasures bee taken of fallible thinges, there- | fore it [C7] foloweth that they be but delusions and shadowes. What woulde you say furthermore, if you saw a man so deceaued 5 with sorcerie and also other detestable witchecraftes, eat, drynke, leap, laugh, yea, and clappe handes for ioye, when ther wer no such thyng there in very dede, as he beleueth he seeth. *Spu.* I wolde say he were both mad and miserable. *Hedo.* I my self haue been often in place, where the lyke thyng 10 hath been doone. There was a priest whiche knewe perfectly by longe experience and practise, the arte to make thynges seme that they were not, otherwise called, *deceptio visus. Sp.* He did not lerne that arte of the holy scripture? *Hedo.* Yea, ra | ther of most popeholy charmes and witchecraftes: that 15 [C7ᵛ] is too saye, of thinges, cursed, dampnable, and wourthy too bee abhorred. Certayne ladies and gentlewomen of the courte, spake vnto hym oftentimes: saiyng, they woulde coom one day too his house and see what good chere he kept: reprouyng, greatly vile and homly fare, and moderate ex- 20 penses in all thynges. He graunted they shulde bee welcome, and very instauntly desired them. And they came fastyng because they would haue better appetites. Whan they wer set to dyner (as it was thought) ther wanted noo kynde of delitious meat: they filled them selues haboundantly: after 25 the feast was | doone, they gaue moost hearty thanckes, for [C8] their galaunte cheare, and departed, euery one of them vnto their owne lodgynges: but anone their stomackes beganne too waxe an hungred, they maruayled what this shuld meane, so soone to be an hungred and a thirste, after so sumptuous a 30 feast: at the last the matter was openly knowen and laught

13 *visus.*] *visus,*
14 scripture?] *exclamation as in* 91:28
*19 coom] coom̄

---

19 coom] The complementary infinitive, *coom̄*, shows a nonfunctional tittle (see 81:6 and note).

at. *Spu.* Not without a cause, it had been muche better for them too haue satisfied their stomackes at their owne chambers with a messe of potage, then to obe fed so delitiousli with vain illusions. *H.* And as I think the commune sort of
5 men ar muche more too bee laught at, whiche in steede of
[C8ᵛ] Godlye thynges, | chose vaine and transitory shadowes, and reioyce excedyngly in suche folishe phansies that turne not afterwarde in too a laughter, but into euerlasting lamentation and sorow. *Spudeus.* The more nerelier I note your
10 saiynges, the better I like them. *Hedo.* Go too, let vs graunt for a tyme these thynges too bee called pleasaunt, that in very dede ar not. Would yow saye that meeth were swete: whiche had more Aloes myngled with it, then honye? *Spud.* I woulde not so say and if there were but the third part of an
15 ounce of Aloes mixt with it. *Hedo.* Orels, would you wishe to bee scabbed because you haue some pleasure too scratch?
[D1] *Spud.* Noo, if I wer | in my right mynd. *HED.* Then weigh with your self how great peyne is intermyngled wyth these false and wrongly named pleasures, that vnshamefast loue,
20 filthie desire, much eatyng and drinking bring vs vnto: I doo omitte now that, which is principall grudge of conscience, enemitie betwixt God and man, and expectation of euerlastyng punishement. What kynd of pleasure, I pray you is ther in these thinges, that dooeth not bryng with it a greate
25 heape of outeward euilles? *SPV.* What bee thei? *HEDO.* We ought to let passe and forbeare in this place auarice, ambition, wrath, pryde, enuy, whiche of their selues bee heuy
[D1ᵛ] and sorowful euylles and | let vs conferre and compare all

8 a] a | a
9 *Spudeus.*] *Spudeus*
19 loue,] loue
*23 punishement] pu-|nishēment
27 pryde,] pryde

---

23 punishement] The tittle in *pu-|nishēment* is apparently nonfunctional. *OED* records no variant spelling with a double 'm'. In *The Epicure*, variant spellings of *punishement*, 98:7–8 and 106:15, are: *punishment*, 101:19–20; *punyshment*, 101:24; *punyshemente*, 108:28.

those thynges together, that haue the name of some chief
and special pleasure: wher as the agew, the hedache, the
swelling of the belly, dulnes of witte, infamy, hurt of memory,
vomyting, decaye of stomacke, tremblyng of the body suc-
cede of ouer muche drynking: thynke you, that the *Epicure* 5
would haue estemed any suche lyke pleasure as thys, conuenient and wourthy desire? *SPV.* He woulde saye it wer vtterly too bee refused. *HEDONI.* Wheras young men also with
hauntynge of whores (as it is dayly seene) catche the newe
leprosie, nowe otherwyse named Iobs agew, and some cal 10
it the scabbes of Naples, throughe | which desease they feele [D2]
often the most extreme and cruell paines of deathe euen in
this lyfe, and cary about abodye resemblyng very much
some dead coarse or carryn, do you thynke that thei apply
them selues vnto godlye pleasure. *SPVD.* Noo, for after thei 15
haue been often familiar with their pretyones, then they
must goo streighte too the barbours, that chaunceth con-
tinuallye vnto all whoremongers. *HED.* Now fayne that ther
wer alyke measure of pain and plesure, would ye then require too haue the toothache so longe as the pleasure of 20
quaffing and whordome endured? *SPV.* Verely I had rather
want them booth, for ther is no commoditie nor van- | tage [D2ᵛ]
to bye pleasure with payn but only to chaung one thing for
another, but the best choise is nowe not too affectionate anye
such leudnes, for *MAR. Tullius* calleth that an inward greife 25
and sorow. *He.* But now the prouocation and entisement of
vnleful plesure, besides that it is much lesse then the pain

2 agew,] agew

8 *HEDONI*] *HEDONi*

*27 plesure F] pleasure HD

---

27 plesure] The variation between readings at the right margin of
Grafton's line 8 (with rearranged spacing throughout the line—not shown
in this reprint), is apparently a stop-press alteration for the purpose of
justifying the line. At p. 97, lines 13 and 14, the Folger copy shows later
states of presswork than the Harvard copy (see the table of press variants,
p. 70). Unlike the two other corrected states in the outer forme of D, there
is no evidence that *plesure* departs from what the translator wrote.

which it bringeth with it, it is also a thing of a very short
time: but if the leprosye bee ones caught, it tourmenteth
men al their life daies very pitifully and oftentimes con-
straineth them to wyshe for death before thei can dye. *SP.*
5 Such disciples as those then, the *Epicure* would not knowe.
HED. For the most part pouertie, a very miserable and
[D3] painfull burden, foloweth | lechery, of immoderate lust com-
meth the palsie, tremblyng of the senewes, bleardnes of eyes,
and blyndnes, the leprosie and not these only, is it not a
10 proper pece of worke (I pray you) to chaung this short
pleasure neyther honest nor yet godly, for so manye euylles
far more greuouse and of muche longer continuance. *SP.* Although there shoulde no pain com of it, I esteme hym to bee
a very fond occupier, which would chaunge precious stones
15 for glasse. *HE.* You meane that would lose the godly pleasures of the mynde, for the coloured pleasures of the body.
SP. That is my meanyng. *HE.* But nowe let vs come to a
[D3ᵛ] more perfecter supputation, neither the agewe | nor yet
pouerty foloweth alwaies carnal pleasure, nor the new leprosy
20 or els the palsy wait not on at altimes the great and excessiue
vse of lecherye, but grudge of consience euermore is a folower
and sure companion of al vnleaful pleasure, then the which
as it is plainly agreed betwixt vs, nothyng is more miserable.
SPV. Yea, rather it grudgeth their conscience sometyme be-
25 fore hande, and in the self pleasure it pricketh their mynde,
yet ther bee some that you woulde say, want this motion
and feelyng. *HE.* Thei bee nowe therfore in worse estate and
condition. Who would not rather feele payne, then too haue hys
body lacke any perfecte sense, truly from some ether intem-
[D4]30 pe- | ratnes of euel desires, euen like as it were a certayne
kynde of drunkenes, or els wont and commune haunt of vice
which ar so hardened in them, that they take a way the
felyng and consideration of euyl in their youth, so that whan
agee commeth vpon them beside other infinitie hurtes and
35 perturbations agaynst whose commyng thei should haue
layd vp the deedes of their former lyfe, as a special iuwel
and treasure: then thei stande greatly in fear of death, a
thyng emongist all other most ineuitable, and that no man

canne shonne: yea, and the more they haue heretofore been
dysmayed and lacked their sences, the greater now is their
vnquietnes and grudge of cons- | cience, then truely the [D4ᵛ]
mynde is sodenly awaked whether it wol or noo, and verely
wher as olde agee is alwayes sad and heuy of it selfe for as 5
muche as it is in subiection and bondage vnto many incommodities of nature, but then it is farre more wretchede and
also fylthye, if the mynde vnquiet with it selfe shal trouble
it also: feastes, ryotous banketyng, syngyng, and daunsynge,
with manye suche other wanton toyes and pastimes which 10
he was communely yeouen vnto and thought very plesaunt
when he was young, bee nowe paynfull vnto hym beyng olde
and crooked: ne agee hath nothyng too comforte and fortifi |
him selfe withall, but onely too remembre that he hath [D5]

*13 crooked: HD] crooked, F

*14 him selfe withall, but onely too remembre that he HD] it selfe
withall, but onely too remembre that it F [*catchword* hym]

---

13 crooked:] Because the 'incorrect correction' at line 14 establishes
that the outer forme of sheet D in the Folger copy is a later state of
wording with respect to the Harvard copy, the Folger punctuation here
in line 13 is likewise apparently a later state in the pressroom. But because sixteenth-century Latin editions have the colon (e.g., BB, E483, sig.
2B2), and because the translator may have preserved the colon in English,
the Folger punctuation probably departs (as does the Folger wording at
line 14) from the punctuation in the lost manuscript from which type was
set. (Leiden edition, I, 885E, has a comma.)

14 him selfe withall, but onely too remembre that he] The most likely
explanation of the disagreement between the catchword *hym* on D4ᵛ
and the pronouns on lines 1–2 of D5 in the Folger copy rests on the authority of the catchword. (For a discussion of the principle drawn upon
here, see R. B. McKerrow, "The Use of the Galley in Elizabethan Printing," *The Library*, 4th ser., II, 97–108, especially 100–101.) The problem
is in part one of style. Throughout a sustained passage in the Latin, Erasmus evokes the dramatic possibilities of *age* (*senectus, animus, senex, aetas,
senecta*) both as a grievous condition of the body and as an old man endur-
ing that condition. (See Leiden edition, I, 885D–E.) The two English
pronouns are mixed in the long sentence in question: the pronoun *it*, re-
ferring to *age*, lines 5–9, shifts to the masculine gender, line 11 through
p. 98, line 5; *i.e.*, just before and after the lines that troubled Grafton's
pressmen. (Compare, also, a similar use of both impersonal and personal
pronouns for *age*, 108:19–28.)

By the simplest and most probable reconstruction, the catchword *hym*

passed ouer the course of yeares in vertue and godly liuyng
and conceaue a special trust too obtaine herafter a better
kynde of life. These be the two staues wherevpon age is
stayed, and if in their steed you wyll lay on hym these two
5 burdens: that is, memorie how synfully he hath ledde his
life, and desperation of the felicitie that is too coome, I praye
you what liuyng thyng can bee feyned too suffre sorer punishement and greater miserie? *Spu.* Verely I can see nothyng
although some man woulde saye an olde horse. *Hedo.* Then
10 to conclude it is too late to waxe wise. And that saiyng ap-
[D5ᵛ] pereth now | too bee very true. Carefull mornynges doo
oftentymes folowe mery euentides, and all vayne and outragious mirth euer turneth into sorowfull sighes: yea, and
they shulde haue considered both that there is noo pleasure
15 aboue the ioyfulnes of the heart, and that chearefull mynde
maketh agee too florishe, an heauy spirit consumeth the
boones, and also that all the dayes of the poore are euell:
that is, sorowfull and wretched. And agayne a quiet mynde
is lyke a contynuall feaste. *SPVDEVS.* Therfore they bee
20 wyse, that thryue in tyme, and gather too gether necessaries

*8 miserie? *Spu*] miserie?. *spu*
9 *Hedo*] *hedo*
10 wise.] wise
17 of the] of fhe

---

on D4ᵛ represents the reading of the manuscript from which type was set,
as do *him* ('i' substituted for 'y') and *he* seen in lines 1–2 of the Harvard
copy. I attribute the stop-press alterations of *him* and *he* to the impersonal
pronouns *it* and *it* seen in the Folger copy to a proofreader's dissatisfaction
with accepting the subject of *age* in the immediate context of D5 as per-
sonified—although proof could have been read on D4ᵛ and D5 at the same
time, as both pages belong to the same forme.

Whereas outer D in the Folger copy is technically a "corrected" forme—
with respect to its later state in the pressroom—the "uncorrected" readings of the Harvard copy in D5 conform more nearly to the lost manuscript
from which type was set. Therefore, uncorrected *him* HD and *he* HD are
the pronouns adopted.

8 miserie? *Spu*] Although "Rentes," fol. 5, line 14, *yeares?.* has the same
double punctuation, it is normalized in this reprint.

for that agee coometh. *HEDONI.* The holy scripture in-
treateth not soo wordely | as too measure the felicitie and [D6]
highe consolation of manne, by the goodes of fortune, onely
he is very poore, that is destitute and voyde of al grace and
vertue, and standeth in boundage and debette, bothe of 5
bodye and solle vnto that tyranne oure moost foo and mortall enemie the deuill. *SPV.* Surely he is one that is veri
rigorous and impatient in demaundynge of his dutie. *HE.*
Moreouer that man is ryche, whiche fyndeth mercye and
foryeouenes at the handes of god. What shuld he feare, that 10
hath suche a protectour? Whether men? where as playnely
theyr hole power may lesse do agaenst God, then the bytyng
of a gnat, | hurteth the Elephant. Whether death? truly that [D6ᵛ]
is a right passage for good men vnto all sufficient ioy and perfection accordyng too the iust reward of true religion and 15
vertue. Whether hell? For as in that the holy prophete
speaketh boldely vnto God. Although I shulde walke in the
middest of the shadow of death, I wil not feare any euils because thou art with me. Wherfore shulde he stande in feare
of deuils, whiche beareth in his heart hym, that maketh the 20
deuils too tremble and quake. For in diuers places the holye
scripture praiseth and declareth openly the mynde of a vertuous man, too bee the right temple of God. And this to bee
so true that | it is not too bee spoken agaynst, ne in any wise [D7]
shuld bee denied. *SPV.* Forsoth I can not see, by what reason 25
these saiynges of yours can be confuted al thoughe they seme
too varye muche from the vulgar and commune opinion of
men. *HEDO.* Why doo they soo? *SPV.* After your reason-
yng euery honest poore man, shulde liue a more pleasaunt life,
then any other, how much soeuer he did habound in riches, 30
honour, and dignitie: and breuely though he had all kynde
of pleasures. *HE.* Adde this too it (if it please you) too bee a

*1 coometh] coom̄
24 that | it] ẙ | that it [*catchword* that]

1 coometh] Because all verbs in the third person singular present indicative in Gerrard's writings show the endings *-eth*, *-th*, or *-the*, I have
emended to conform.

kyng, yea, or an emperour if you take away a quiet mynd
with it selfe, I dare boldely say, that the poore man sklender-
[D7ᵛ] lye | and homely appareled, made weake with fastyng,
watchyng, great toile and labour, and that hath scarcely a
5 groat in all the worlde, so that his mynde bee godly, he
lyueth more deliciously then that man whiche hathe fyue
hundreth times greater pleasures and delicates, then euer
had *Sardanapalus*. *SP.* Why is it then, that we see communely those that bee poore looke farre more heuely then riche
10 men? *HED.* Because some of them bee twise poore, eyther
some desease, nedines, watchyng, labour, nakednesse, doo soo
weaken the state of their bodyes, that by reason therof, the
chearefulnes of their myndes neuer sheweth it selfe, neyther
[D8] in these thin- | ges, nor yet in their deathe. The mynde, for-
15 sooth thoughe it bee inclosed within this mortal bodye, yet
for that it is of a stronger nature, it somwhat transfourmeth
and fascioneth the bodie after it selfe, especially if the vehement instigation of the spirit approche the violent inclina-
tion of nature: this is the cause we see oftentymes suche
20 men as bee vertuous die more cherefully, then those that
make pastyme contynually, and bee yeouen vnto al kynd of
pleasures. *SP.* In very dede, I haue meruayled oftten at that
thyng. *HED.* Forsoothe it is not a thyng too bee marueyled
[D8ᵛ] at, though that there shulde bee vnspeakeable | ioy and
25 comforte where God is present, whiche is the heed of all
mirth and gladnes, nowe this is no straunge thyng, althoughe
the mynde of a godly man doo reioyce contynually in this
mortall bodye: where as if the same mynde or spirit discend-
ed into the lowest place of hell shuld lose no parte of felicitie,
30 for whersoeuer is a pure mynd, there is god, wher God is:

*10 men? HD] men. F
23 *HED.*] *HED*
25 is present] is | is present

---

10 men?] Latin readings show the question mark (*BB*, E483, sig.
2B2ᵛ; Leiden edition, I, 886C). The Harvard reading here in D7ᵛ improves
the punctuation given by the Folger copy, making the inner forme of
sheet D a corrected forme.

there is paradise, ther is heauen, ther is felicitie, wher felicitie
is: ther is the true ioy and synsere gladnes. *SP*. But yet they
shuld liue more pleasauntly, if certein incommodities were
taken from them, and had suche pastymes as eyther they
dispise orels can not get nor attaine vnto. *HE*. | (I praye you) 5[E1]
doo you meane, suche incommodities as by the commune
course of nature folow the condition or state of man: as hun-
ger, thirst, desease, werynes, age, death, lyghtnyng yearth-
quake, fluddes and battail? *SPV*. I meane other, and these
also. *HEDO*. Then we intreate styll of mortal thynges and 10
not of immortal, and yet in these euils the state of vertuous
men, may bee better borne withal, then of suche as seeke for
the pleasures of the body they care not howe. *SPV*. Why so?
HEDO. Especyally because their myndes bee accustomed
and hardened with most sure and moderate gouernaunce of 15
reason against al outragious affections of the mind | and they [E1ᵛ]
take more patiently those thynges that cannot bee shonned
then the other sort doo. Furthermore, for as muche as thei
perceiue, all such thynges ar sent of god, either for the punish-
ment of their faultes, or els too excitate and sturre them vp 20
vnto vertue, then thei as meeke and obediente chyldren receiue
them from the hand of their mercifull father, not only de-
sireously, but also chearefully and geue thankes also, namely
for so merciful punyshment and inestimable gaines. *SPV*.
But many doo occation griefes vnto them selues. *HEDO*. But 25
mo seeke remedye at the *Phisicions*, either to preserue their
bodies in helth or elles if they bee sycke, too re- | couer [E2]
health, but willyngly too cause their owne sorowes, that is,
pouertie, sickenes, persecution, slaunder, excepte the loue of
God compel vs therto, it is no vertue but folishnes: but as 30
often as thei bee punyshed for Christ and iustice sake, who
dar bee so bold as too cal them beggers and wretches? whan
the Lord himself very famyliarly calleth them blessed, and
commaundeth vs to reioyse for their state and condition.

18 doo.] doo
30 no vertue] no- | vertue
31 often] of- | often

SPV. Neuerthelesse, these thynges haue a certayne payne and griefe. *HEDO*. Thei haue, but on the onesyde, what for fear of hel, and the other for hoope of euerlastynge ioye, the payne is sone past and forgotten. Now tell me if you knewe [E2ʳ] 5 that | you myghte neuer bee sycke, or elles that you shoulde feele no payne of your body in your life tyme, if you woulde but ones suffer your vtter skinne too bee prycked with a pynnes puinct, would you not gladly and with all your very heart suffer then so lytle a payne as that is? *SPV*. 10 Verye gladlye, yea, rather if I knewe perfectlye that my teeth would neuer ake, I would willynglye suffer too bee prycked depe with a nedle, and too haue both mine eares bored through with a bodkin. *HEDO*. Surely what payne soeuer happeneth in this lyfe, it is lesse and shorter, com- 15 pared with the eternall paines, then is the soden pricke of a [E3] needle, incomparison of the | lyfe of man though it bee neuer so long, for there is no conuenience or proportion of the thyng that hath ende, and that whych is infinite. *SPV*. You speake very truly. *HEDO*. Now if a man coulde fully perswade you, 20 that you should neuer feele payne in al your life, if you did but ones deuide the flame of the fyre, with your hande, whyche thyng vndoughtely *Pithagoras* forbade, woulde you not gladlye doo it? *SPV*. Yea, on that condicion I had liefer doo it an hundred times, if I knew precisely the promiser 25 would kepe touch. *HE*. It is playne God cannot deceaue. But now that feelyng of paine in the fyre is longer vnto the whole [E3ʳ] lyfe of man, then is the | lyfe of man, in respect of the heauenlye ioye, althoughe it were thrise so long as the yeares of *Nestor*, for that casting of the hand in the fyre thoughe it 30 bee neuer so shorte, yet it is some parte of hys lyfe, but the whole lyfe of man is noo portion of tyme in respect of the eternal lyfe. *SPV*. I haue nothyng too saye against you. *HEDO*. Doo you then thyncke that anye affliction or tourment can disquiet those that prepare them selues wyth a 35 chearful hearte and a stedfast hoope vnto the kyngedome of

4 forgotten.] forgottē
9 *SPV*.] *SPV*
32 lyfe.] lyfe,

God, wher as the course of this lyfe is nowe so shorte?
SPVDE. I thinke not, if thei haue a sure perswasion and a
constant hope too attayne it. *HEDO.* I coome | now vnto [E4]
those pleasures, whiche you obiected agaynst me, they do
wythdrawe them selues from daunsynge, bankettynge, from 5
pleasaunte seeghtes, they dispyce all these thynges, as thus:
for to haue the vse of thinges farre more ioyfulle, and haue
as great pleasure as these bee, but after another sorte: the
eye hath not seene, the eare hath not heard, nor the heart of
man cannot thyncke what consolations *GOD* hathe ordeined 10
for them that loue hym. Sayncte Paule knewe what maner of
thynges shoulde bee the songes, queeres, daunsynges, and
bankettes of vertuous myndes, yea, in this lyfe. *SPVDEVS.*
but there bee some leafull plea- | sures, whyche they vtter- [E4ᵛ]
lye refuse. *HEDONIVS.* That maye bee, for the immoderate 15
vse of leafull and godly games or pastymes, is vnleaful: and
if you wyll excepte this one thing onlye, in al other thei ex-
celle whiche seeme too leade a paynfull lyfe, and whom we
take too bee ouerwhelmed with all kynd of miseries. Now I
prai you what more roialler sight can ther be, then the con- 20
templation of this world? and such men as the be in fauour
of god keping his holy commaundementes and loue his most
blessed testament, receiue far greater pleasure in the syght
therof, then thother sorte doo, for while thei behold wyth
ouercurious eyes, that wonderful worke, their mynde | is 25[E5]
troubled because they can not compasse for what purpose
he doeth such thinges, then thei improue the moost righte and
wise gouernour of all and murmour at his doinges as though
they were goddes of reprehension: and often finde faute with
that lady nature, and saye that she is vnnaturall, whiche 30
taunt forsooth with as muche spite as can bee shewed with
woordes, greueth nature: but truely it redoundeth on hym,
that made nature, if there bee any at all. But the vertuous

13 *SPVDEVS.*] *SPVDEVS*
*21 the] y̆

---

21 the] *the* is a relative pronoun (see *OED*).

man with godly and simple eyes beholdeth with an excedyng
reioyce of heart the workes of his Lorde and father highly
[E5ᵛ] praysyng them all, and neither reprehendeth nor | findeth
faut with any of them, but for euery thyng yeoueth moste
5 hearty thankes, when he considereth that al were made for
the loue of man. And so in all thynges, he praieth vnto the
infinite power, deuine wisedome, and goodnes of the maker,
wherof he perceiueth moste euident tokens in thynges that
bee here created. Now fain that there were suche a palace in
10 verie deede as *Apuleus* faineth, or els one that were more
royall and gorgeouse, and that you shoulde take twoo thither
with you too beholde it, the one a straunger, whiche gooeth
for this intent onely too see the thyng, and the other the
seruaunt or soonne of hym that firste causeth this buyldyng,
[E6]15 whether | will haue more delectie in it? the straunger, too
whom suche maner of house dooeth nothyng appartain, or the
soonne whiche beholdeth with greate ioye and pleasure, the
witte, riches, and magnificence of his deerely beloued father,
especially when he dooeth consider all this worke was made
20 for his sake. *Sp.* Your question is too plain: for they most
communely that bee of euill condicions, knowe that heauen
and all thinges contained therin, were made for mannes sake.
HEDO. Almoste al knowe that, but some dooe not remembre
it, shewyng them selues vnthankeful for the great and exhu-
25 berant benefittes of god, and al though thei remember it, yet
[E6ᵛ] that man taketh | greater delight in the sight of it whiche
hath more loue vnto the maker therof, in like maner as, he
more chearfully wyll behold the element whiche aspireth towarde the eternall life. *SPV.* Your saiynges are muche like
30 too bee true. *HED.* Nowe the pleasures of feastes dooeth not
consist in the delicates of the mouth, nor in the good sauces
of cookes, but in health of body and appetite of stomacke.
You may not thynke that any delicious person suppeth more
pleasauntly hauyng before hym partriches, turtelles, leuer-
35 ettes, bekers, sturgeon, and lamprayes: then a vertuous man
hauyng nothing too eat, but onely bread potage, or wortes:
[E7] and nothyng | too drynke, but water, single bere, or wyne
well alayde, be cause he taketh these thinges as prepared of

God vnto all lyuyng creatures, and that they bee now yeouen
vnto him of his gentyll and mercifull father, praier maketh
euery thyng too sauour well. The petition in the begynnyng
of dyner sanctifieth all thynges and in a while after there is
recited some holy lesson of the woorde of God: whiche more 5
refresheth the minde, then meate the body, and grace after all
this. Finally he riseth from the table, not ful: but recreated,
not laden, but refreshed: yea, refreshed both in spirit and
bodie, thynke you that any chief deuiser of these muche vsed
bankets, and | deintye delicaces fareth nowe more delicious- 10 [E7ᵛ]
ly? *Spudeus.* But in *Venus* there is greate delectacions if we
beleue *Arestotell.* *Hed.* And in this behalfe the vertuous manne
far excelleth as well as in good fare, weigh you now the matter as it is, the better a manne loueth his wife, the more he
delecteth in the good fellowship and familiaritie that is be- 15
twene theim after the course of nature. Furthermore, no
menne loue their wiues more vehemently then thei that loue
theim euen soo, as Christ loued the churche. For thei that
loue them for the desire of bodely pleasure, loue them not.
More ouer, the seldomer any man dooeth accompany with 20
his wife, the greater pleasure, it | is to hym afterwarde, and [E8]
that thyng the wanton poete knew full well whiche writeth,
rare and seldome vse stereth vp pleasures. Albeit, the lest
parte of pleasure is in the familiare company betwene theim.
There is forsothe far greater in the continuall leadyng of their 25
liues too gether, whiche emongest none can be so plesaunt
as those that loue syncerely and faithfully together in godly
and christian loue, and loue a like one the other. In the other
sort, often when the pleasure of the body decaieth and waxeth
old loue waxeth coold and is sone forgotton, but emongest 30
right christen men, the more that the lust of the flesh de-

11 *Spudeus*] S*Pudeus*
13 weigh] wiegh
*17 loue their] louē their

---

17 loue their] I have disregarded the tittle in *louē* because no inflected
form of a verb in the third person plural present indicative occurs in Gerrard's writings to support such a reading as *louen.*

creaseth and vanisheth away, the more then al godly loue
[E8ᵛ] encreseth. | Are you not yet perswaded that none lyue more
pleasauntly then they whiche liue continually in vertue and
true religion of god? *SP*. Would god all men were as well per-
5 swaded in that thyng. *He*. And if they bee Epicures that lyue
pleasauntli: none bee righter Epicures then they that liue
vertuously, and if we wyll that euery thyng haue it right
name none deserueth more the cogname of an Epicure, then
that Prince of all godly wisedome too whom most reuerently
10 we ought alwaies too praye: for in the greeke tonge an Epicure signifieth an helper. Nowe whan the lawe of nature was
first corrupted with sinne, when the law of Moses did rather
[F1] prouoke euil desires then | remedy them. Whan the ty-
raunte Sathanas reygned in this worlde freely and wythout
15 punishement, then thys prynce onely, dyd sodenlye helpe
mankynde redy to perishe: wherfore thei erre shamefully
which scoff and bable that *CHRIST* was one that was sadd
and of a malancolye nature, and that he hath prouoked vs
vnto an vnpleasaunt kynde of lyfe, for onely he did shewe a
20 kind of liuing most godly and fullest of al true pleasure, if
we might haue the stone of *Tantalus* taken awaye from vs.
SPVD. What darke saiyng is this? *HEDO*. It is a mery tale
too laugh at, but this bourd induceth verye graue and sadde
[F1ᵛ] thynges. *SPV*. I tary too heare | this mery conceite, that
25 you name too bee so sage a matter. *HE*. Thei whiche gaue
their studye and diligence to colour and setfurth the preceptes
of Philosophie wyth subtil fables, declare that there was one
Tantalus broughte vnto the table of the goddes, whych was
euer furnished wyth all good fare, and most nete and sumptu-
30 ous that myght bee, whan thys straunger shoulde take hys
leaue, Iupyter thought it was for his great liberalitie and
highe renoume, that his guest shuld not depart wythout
some rewarde, he wylled him therfore too aske what he

2 encreseth.] encreseth
13 then | remedy] thē | then remedy [*catchword* reme]
22 *HEDO*] *EDO*
25 *HE*.] *HE*

woulde, and he shoulde haue it: *Tantalus* (forsooth) lyke a
verye leude and foolyshe person, | for that he sette all the [F2]
felicitie and pleasure of man in the delectation of the bely,
and glotonye, desired but only too sytte at suche a table all
the dayes of hys life, Iupiter graunted him his desire, and 5
shortly his vow was there stablished and ratifyed. *Tantalus*
nowe sytteth at the table furnyshed wyth all kindes of delicates, such drinke as the goddes druncke of was set on the
table, and there wanted no rooses nor odours that could
yeoue any swete smel before the Goddes, *Ganymedes* the 10
buttler or one lyke vnto hym, standeth euer redye, the
Muses stande rounde aboute syngyng pleasauntly, mery
Silenus daunseth, ne ther wanted noo fooles | too laugh at, [F2ᵛ]
and breuely, there was euerye thynge that coulde delyght
any sence of man, but emongist all these, *Tantalus* sytteth 15
all sadde, syghyng, and vnquiet with hym selfe, neither
laughing nor yet touching such thynges as were set before
hym. *SPVDE*. What was the cause? *HED*. Ouer his head as
he sate there hanged by an heere a great stone euer lyke too
fall. *SPV*. I woulde then haue conueied my selfe from suche 20
a table. *HEDO*. But his vowe had bound hym too the con-
trarye, for Iupyter is not so easye too intreate as oure *GOD*,
which dooeth vnloose the pernitious vowes of menne, that
bee made contrary vnto his holy woord, if thei bee | penitent [F3]
and sorye therfore, or elles it myght bee thus, the same 25
stoone that woulde not suffer hym too eate, would neither
suffer hym to ryse, for if he had but ones moued he shuld
haue been quashed al in peeses with the fall thereof. *SPVDE*.
You haue shewed a very mery fable. *HEDON*. But nowe
heare that thing, which you wil not laugh at: the commune 30
people seeke too haue a pleasaunt life in out warde thynges,
where as noothyng can yeoue that, but onely a constant and

14 there was] there | there was
15 man,] mā
18 hym.] hym
21 *HEDO*.] *HEDO*
29 fable.] fable

〖*107*〗

a quiet mind: for surely a far heuier stone hangeth ouer these
that grudge with them selues, then hanged ouer *Tantalus:*
[F3ᵛ] it only hangeth not ouer them, but greueth and op- | presseth
the mynde, ne the mind is not troubled wyth any vayn
5 hoope, but looketh euery houre to bee caste in too the paynes
of hell, I praye you what can bee so pleasaunt emongist all
thinges that bee yeouen vnto man, that coulde reioyse the
mynde, whyche were oppressed wyth suche a stoone?
SPVDE. Truely there is nothyng but madnes, or elles in-
10 credulitie. *HEDO.* Yf younge menne woulde weygh these
thynges, that bee quyckly prouoked and entised with pleasure as it were wyth the cuppe of *Circes,* whiche in steade
of theyr greatest pleasures receiue poysone myxte wyth
honye. Howe circumspecte would they bee too doo anye
[F4] 15 thynge vnad- | uisedly that shoulde grudge their mindes
afterward? What thinge is it that thei would not doo too
haue suche a godly treasure in store against their latter daies?
that is a minde knowyng it selfe cleane and honest and a
name that hath not been defiled at any time. But what thyng
20 now is more miserable then is agee? Whan it beholdeth, and
loketh backward on thinges that be past seeth plainly with
great grudg of conscience howe fayre thynges he hathe de-
spiced and sette lyght by, (that is, howe farre he hath discent-
ed and gone astray from the promyses made vnto God in
25 baptime) and agayn, how foule and noughty thinges he hath
[F4ᵛ] clipped and enbraced, and whan | hee looketh forwarde, hee
seeth then the daye of iudgemente drawe neere, and shortely
after the eternall punyshemente of hell. *SPVDE.* I esteme
theim most happie whych haue neuer defyled theyr youthe,
30 but euer haue increased in vertu, til thei haue coomne vnto
the last puincte of age. *HEDO.* Next them thei ar too bee
commended that haue wythdrawne theim selues from the
folie of youth in tyme. *SPVDE.* But what councel wil you
yeoue agee that is in suche great myserie. *HEDO.* No man
35 shoulde dispayre so long as life endureth, I wyl exhorte him
to flee for helpe vnto the infinitie mercye and gentilnes of

28 of hell] of | of hell

God. *SP.* But the longer that he hath liued | the heape of [F5]
his synnes hath euer waxen greate and greater, so that nowe
it passeth the nomber of the sandes in the sea. *HE.* But the
mercies of our lord far excede those sandes, for although the
sande can not bee numbred of manne, yet hit hath an ende, 5
but the mercie of God neither knoweth ende, ne measure.
SP. Yea but he hath no space that shall dye by and by.
HEDONI. The lesse tyme he hath the more feruently he
should cal vnto god for grace, that thyng is long inough before God, whiche is of suche power as too ascende from the 10
yearth vnto heauen, for a short prayer forsoth streght en-
treth heauen, if it bee made with a vehement spirit. It is
written, that | the woman synner spoken of in the gospell [F5ᵛ]
did penaunce al her life dayes: but with how fewe wordes
again did the thief obtain Paradise in the houre of death? If 15
he will crye with hearte and mynde, God haue mercie on me
after thy great mercie: God wil take awaye from hym *Tanta-*
lus stone and yeoue in his hearyng ioye and comfort and his
bones humiled throughe contrition, wil reioyse that he hath his
synnes for yeouen hym. 20

FINIS. |

Imprinted at London within the [F6]
precinct of the late dissolued house
of the gray Friers, by Richarde
Grafton, Printer too the 25
Princes grace.
the .XXIX.
daie of Iuly, the yere
of our Lorde.
M. D. XLV.

3 sea. *HE.*] sea, *HE*
7 by.] by,
27 *the .XXIX.*] *the. XXIX.*

Facsimile of block on sig. F6ᵛ of *The Epicure*. Original, 68 × 49 mm.
By permission of the Folger Shakespeare Library.

Facsimile of device on sig. F7 of *The Epicure*. Original, 68 × 49 mm.
By permission of the Folger Shakespeare Library.

Staton, Jr., and Abraham Fraunce's Translation, *The Lamentations of Amyntas*, edited by Franklin M. Dickey, 1967.

Second Series

Vol. III. *The dyaloge called Funus*, A Translation of Erasmus's Colloquy (1534), & *A very pleasaunt & fruitful Diologe called The Epicure*, Gerrard's Translation of Erasmus's Colloquy (1545), edited by Robert R. Allen, 1969.

Vol. IV. *Leicester's Ghost*, edited by Franklin B. Williams, Jr., *in press*.